AIRGUN SHOOTING

An Introduction

Les Herridge

A & C Black · London

First published 1987 by
A & C Black (Publishers) Limited
35 Bedford Row, London WC1R 4JH

Herridge, Les
  Airgun shooting: an introduction.
  1. Shooting   2. Air guns
  I. Title
  799.3'12   GV1174
  ISBN 0-7136-5604-2

ISBN 0 7136 5604 2

Typeset by August Filmsetting, Haydock, St Helens
Printed and bound in Great Britain by
Butler & Tanner Ltd,
Frome and London

CONTENTS

FOREWORD

Considering how many people own an airgun, and how many more take up the sport for the first time each year, it has always surprised me that there has never been a book which offers a sound, down-to-earth introduction to airgun shooting. Les Herridge has now put that right, and this book provides all the basic information that newcomers to airgunning need to know.

His advice on how to choose and use an airgun as well as his clear explanations of the airgun safety code and law are essential reading for anyone picking up a gun for the first time. A great deal of what he says will be valued by experienced shooters, too, for it is all too easy to forget some of the more fundamental points as the years drift by.

Les Herridge has been a keen airgun shooter for nearly thirty years, and his articles have appeared in several airgun magazines and earned him a deserved following. In particular, I think, he has that happy knack of keeping things simple where another writer might make it complicated.

Youngsters of all ages will be able to grasp Les's text without difficulty, and I have no doubt they will enjoy this superb sport all the more by following his advice.

If you want to master the basics of airgunning and, most importantly, become a safer shooter, I can only recommend you to study what Les Herridge says and then do your best to put it into practice.

Paul Dobson
Editor of *Air Gunner*

INTRODUCTION

My aim in writing this book has been to answer, in as straightforward a manner as possible, those questions which are commonly raised by newcomers to the sport of airgun shooting. I have tried to cover most aspects, from choosing a gun through to competitive shooting and hunting. I have also outlined the importance of safety and of a mature approach to the sport.

Airgun shooting is a highly enjoyable and relatively inexpensive pastime which is available to a wide age group. It can provide many hours of pleasure and relaxation, and I hope that you will gain as much enjoyment from your shooting as I have done over the years.

Please always remember to act responsibly when you are dealing with guns and so help to maintain the high standards which are being established for this increasingly popular sport.

Acknowledgements

I would like to record my warmest thanks to the following individuals for their assistance in the preparation of this book: John Darling for the fine cover photograph; Paul Dobson, editor of *Airgunner*, for the Foreword; Ian Law for his valuable help with the sections on competitive shooting; Gerald Cardew for his valued advice; David Overland for the illustration on page 7; my father, Syd Herridge, for helping instil in me an early love of the countryside and of shooting; and finally my wife, Janet, for enduring many months of noisy two-fingered typing.

CHAPTER ONE

AIRGUNS:
LAW AND SAFETY

Most of us have seen teenagers on a canal towpath or river bank, happily blasting away with an airgun at tin cans in the water, or shooting at bottles on a council rubbish tip. What we may not have realised is that they were almost certainly breaking the law. The chances are that they did not know it either. Shooting is not permitted in any public place, and a public place may be defined as anywhere the public at large has a legal right to be: pavements, roads, public footpaths, public parks, public car parks, canal towpaths (if they are open to the public), seaside promenades and so on.

The law is intended to protect people from possible injury, so the 'no public places' clause is an eminently sensible one. However, it is one which is frequently ignored, sometimes resulting in accidents, which, apart from their own immediate and often serious consequences, can lead to hysterical cries for the banning of all air weapons, or at least for a tightening of the law involving them. We shall see, though, that the law referring to airguns is already very strict indeed. If it were fully understood accidents would be few, and the sport would be less maligned than it tends to be at present. Be in no doubt, airguns are not toys, and even the relatively low powered examples can cause serious injury, even death, if misused. People have been permanently blinded and paralysed by airgun pellets, and accidents can occur very quickly in an unguarded moment. Always regard your airgun as loaded, whether it is or not, and *never* point a gun at anyone, nor at any animal. It is worth remembering that many people have been injured or even killed by 'unloaded' guns.

A pellet, which is propelled by an airgun or pistol at the relatively low velocity of 300 feet per second, will penetrate into soft wood from quite a considerable distance. Imagine what it will do to human flesh. Although the maximum power of air rifles and pistols is restricted by law to 12 foot pounds muzzle energy and 6 foot pounds energy respectively, a rifle on the legal limit will project a .22 pellet at more than 600 feet per second, or more than 800 feet per second if the rifle is in .177 calibre. Pistol velocities are, naturally, somewhat less, but still above 300 feet per second.

Domestic animals are sometimes shot at by irresponsible people, but often by a gardener who simply wants to dissuade cats from spoiling his

garden. To frighten a cat from his garden, the gardener lets fly with what he believes to be a stinging shot from a low powered air pistol or rifle, and has the satisfaction of seeing the startled animal leap into the air and run away, apparently quite unharmed, but suitably 'warned'. The cat makes its way to a quiet shed where it lies down in a corner and licks at a small hole in its side. A week later, it dies, in the same place, in considerable pain from its wound. The owner, who eventually finds the unfortunate animal, may, understandably, write a vitriolic letter to the local newspaper, decrying the use of airguns. My own pedigree Siamese died in identical circumstances, and my vet informed me that death and injury among domestic pets from airgun misuse is extremely common. If you shoot at any domestic animal you may be breaking more than one law. Cruelty to animals is an obvious offence, but if you are shooting in a public place, that is an additional offence. Shoot across someone else's garden and you still break the law. If you are under age without supervision, yet another offence is committed. Shooting law is very complex, and it is, therefore, very important to understand it clearly to avoid transgression.

Age Restrictions

The law is strict regarding young people and airguns. Boys and girls of all ages can be fascinated by airguns, and often progress from cap guns of childhood to the potential danger of airguns. Statistics indicate that young teenagers are responsible for most of the ill-effects which are the result of the use, or misuse, of airguns.

Children under 14 years are forbidden by law to own an airgun at all, and may only use one if they are supervised by an adult over 21. They are also, like anyone else, prevented from using an airgun in public places. It is worth mentioning that the supervising adult may be held responsible for any misdemeanour committed by the youngster. The principle is not unlike that of a learner driver who needs to be accompanied by an experienced driver, at all times.

Between the ages of 14 and 17 years, youngsters are not legally allowed to buy an airgun or ammunition, but someone over 17, usually their parent, may buy these for them, and then they may shoot unsupervised, provided they are in a place where they have a legal right to be.

Youngsters in this second age group may legally carry an *unloaded* air rifle in a public place, but only if it is in a securely fixed cover and cannot be fired. There are *no* circumstances where a person under the age of 17 years may have possession of an air pistol (even an unloaded one) in public, except in connection with an approved range or shooting gallery.

Trespassing

We have seen that airguns are prohibited from being used in any public place, so it will be apparent that they may only be used on private land or premises, and then only where the shooter has been granted permission to shoot from the owner of the land. Shooting on private land without permission constitutes armed trespass, for which the penalties can be severe. If you are hunting, you may also fall foul of anti-poaching laws and be liable to confiscation of your airgun.

It is worth remembering the simple fact that *all* land is owned by someone. This is a point many people overlook when they see a patch of disused land, or an old abandoned industrial site. The land may not be fenced, and it may be full of rabbits and tempting to a budding hunter, but unless you have permission, preferably in writing, you should not attempt to shoot there. Make an effort to gain the necessary permission beforehand.

Even so-called 'common' land is unsuitable for shooting, since it could technically be regarded as a public place. In areas such as Wales and Scotland, the hills and mountains are often unfenced, and impart the impression that anyone may roam around at will, as indeed walkers and nature lovers often do. But these areas are usually owned by hill farmers, who might well take a dim view of strangers with airguns prowling around among their sheep. The Forestry Commission is another large landowner in Britain, and while its representatives may turn a blind eye to the activities of an airgun enthusiast, it is pointless to take unneccessary chances.

Public Awareness

It is important to remember that the general public has an inbuilt fear of any kind of gun. The sight of a stranger, perhaps clad in pseudo-military camouflage clothing, carrying a sinister looking rifle with a telescopic sight on top, and roaming around on land where he has no right to be, could certainly cause alarm. It could also result in the landowner telephoning the local constabulary, and the trespasser may well find himself invited to the police station to help with further enquiries.

In law, to say that you 'did not know' does not constitute a defence. The best that could be hoped for is that your honest face and appropriate pleading might convince the magistrate that your ignorance is genuine, and *may*, therefore, be taken as a mitigating circumstance. That will not stop you from being found guilty, it may simply reduce the sentence. Expect to have your airgun confiscated, too.

Storing and Transporting an Airgun

The same principle of not alarming the public applies when transporting an airgun. We have looked at what the law says with regard to young people using airguns. The law also makes it clear that people under 17 years of age may only carry an unloaded airgun in public, if it is in a securely fastened gun cover to prevent it from being fired, either accidentally or intentionally. Those under 14 years of age may only carry an airgun in public if they are supervised continuously by an adult over the age of 21, and the aforementioned condition, i.e. that the gun be in a securely fastened cover, is, of course, applicable to under-14s.

As I pointed out earlier, the law is eminently sensible, so far as it applies to air-powered weapons, and the principle of keeping an airgun in a proper cover is just as sensible as the other requirements. If I were driving my car down a busy road in an urban area, and saw several young people carrying uncovered airguns, I should feel a little uneasy myself. Everyone, regardless of age, should keep a gun covered until they are actually in the locality where it is to be used.

General Safety and Security

Safety and security go hand in hand so far as any type of gun is concerned, and airguns which are not actually in use should be carefully stored in a secure place. Airguns should not be used or stored within reach of small children. Youngsters are often fascinated with guns, but unfortunately they have little real concept of what the dangers are, and regard airguns as mere toys. The results of carelessness can and have led to tragedy.

A securely made gun case with a strong lock is the best means of storing guns away from questing little fingers, and will also help to prevent theft. If your airgun collection is quite valuable, you may like to consider having it insured, but you may find that the insurers will insist upon basic security precautions being taken before they will issue a cover note or policy.

When handling any weapon, even a relatively low powered air pistol, always keep it pointed towards the target area, and keep people, particularly children, away from that area. Avoid waving the gun around, especially while you are loading it, and *never* fool about with it. Never run with a loaded gun either – that invites trouble. To give yourself a rough idea of the power of your airgun and, hopefully, a sense of healthy respect for it, place a flat sheet of thick steel against a wall, and fire several lead pellets directly and squarely at it from several metres away. You will find that a high powered air rifle will literally shoot the centres out of the pellets, leaving the remnants totally flattened beyond all recognition. Lower powered airguns produce pellets damaged to varying degrees. Admittedly, lead pellets are quite soft and easily deformed, but just imagine what that deformed pellet would have done to your delicate body if it had hit you. So, handle your airgun accordingly, with the respect it merits.

Safety with regard to Animals

If you are out hunting, keep away from sheep, cattle, horses and pigs, both when actually shooting and, as far as possible, when stalking. Every year farm animals are hit by airgun pellets, often fired deliberately, but occasionally their injuries are the result of sheer carelessness. Apart from the obvious suffering to the animal, and the veterinary bills which might arise, there is also the possibility that the farmers may become alienated against all airgun users, regardless of who they are, or how they act. Farmers will be less encouraged to allow their land to be used for shooting and are also likely to tell the neighbouring landowners about such cases of misuse of airguns. In this way, more potential shooting land is lost to numerous airgun users.

It really is in the interest of the sport for you to report personally to the police any individuals who are seen shooting at farm animals, assuming that you do not feel able to put a stop to it yourself. Just remember that if you shut your eyes to the problem, you devalue your own sport. What is more, those involved will continue to misuse their guns until someone else has the strength of mind to stand up for what they know to be right, by which time a great deal of damage may have been done, both to the animals and to the reputation of the sport. These people certainly have nothing in common with serious airgun users, and they comprise an element which must be severely reprimanded if the sport is to survive in its present form.

Adults have a great part to play in teaching youngsters both about the basic skills of shooting, including safety and careful handling techniques, and the law. The best teacher has always been example, and the attitude of someone who is held in high esteem by a young person will always influence the youngsters far more, for good or bad, than any amount of talking or instruction.

Ammunition

Chapter 3 deals with the setting up of an effective backstop for shooting, but it is worth bearing in mind here that some types of airgun ammunition are inclined to bounce about dangerously, unlike the familiar lead pellets, which tend to expend their energy quickly when they hit a hard surface at right angles. BB shots, airgun darts and some non-lead hunting pellets are the usual culprits. Care should be taken when using these types of ammunition.

Oddly enough, it is often the low powered guns which cause the most dangerous ricochets, as high powered shots usually penetrate or flatten out harmlessly. A shot from a hunting air rifle, for instance, will pierce soft timber at any reasonable range, but a low powered airgun will cause the pellet to bounce off the wood and wend its way back to you – often with painful, or serious, results.

Pistols

With pistols, the question of safety should be given even more consideration than with rifles. Due to their compact size and 'pointability', air pistols could possibly be mistaken for toy guns by youngsters. They should, therefore, always be stored well out of reach of children, and, of course, kept unloaded and uncocked. Because of this 'pointability', pistols are inclined to be angled in all directions while being loaded and prepared for firing. Be extremely cautious and guard against accidental discharges, keeping the weapon pointed towards the target area at all times. Insist that anyone shooting with you does the same.

Safety Catches

I am not a great believer in safety catches on airguns, because my view is that an airgun should not be loaded and cocked unless it is ready to fire, and that is a far better safety device than any mechanical aid. I will concede, however, that safety catches do have an application in hunting, especially when pump-up guns are used. Pump-ups are noisy to cock, requiring several firm pumps, and it is detrimental to the hunting if this operation needs to be done when the quarry has already been sighted, so a safety catch can be useful here. Safety catches are inclined to make people over-confident, leading to forgetfulness of basic precautions. On balance, therefore, it is my personal opinion that we are better off without them.

CHAPTER TWO
CHOOSING AN AIRGUN

Airguns range in price from a few pounds for a very basic pop-out barrelled pistol to several hundred pounds for a top flight match rifle. Between the two extremes there has grown, in recent years, a vast array of apparently similar weapons, making a beginner's choice difficult. Purchasing on impulse, by appearance only, is like a lucky dip, and will usually lead to disappointment. Parents buying for a youngster will often be confused and unsure about where to go for information.

A good gun dealer will offer free advice and will not put any sort of pressure on a potential customer. Many dealers now have their own range where a customer will often have the opportunity of trying several different weapons.

The first step in choosing an airgun is to determine the type of shooting for which the gun is intended. A powerful hunting rifle would

Always seek expert advice when choosing an airgun.

obviously be an unnecessary expense for backyard shooting, apart from being heavy and perhaps a little clumsy in a confined space. Conversely, a low powered pistol or rifle is of little use to a prospective rabbit hunter. Furthermore, a top quality match air rifle is really only suited to competitive target shooting, no matter how attractive it may look in a rack above the mantelpiece.

Another point to remember is that a young person of light build may find a heavy hunting or match rifle very cumbersome to handle. Some powerful air rifles and pistols can be difficult to cock, too, so the golden rule must be 'try it first.'

Value for Money

Having decided upon the type of shooting for which the airgun is most likely to be used, the next consideration for many prospective purchasers must be price. Probably the best plan is to list all the airguns which appear to fit your requirements, bearing in mind that there will still be many air weapons which fall into the 'general purpose' group, and will, with few exceptions, suit many likely applications. Having listed appropriate guns, those which fall outside your price range can then be eliminated.

The most expensive airguns, generally speaking, are of German origin, such as Weihrauch, Feinwerkbau, or Haenel. They are invariably engineered to a very high standard, and often have a well earned reputation throughout the world for quality and reliability. The Weihrauch is particularly renowned for its fine trigger mechanism, which contributes to a high standard of accuracy in these weapons.

At the lower end of the scale, guns from Spain, Eastern Europe and China can be bought quite cheaply. Airguns from Spain are probably the best of these, and the quality of some Spanish airguns is exceptionally good. The Spanish 'Center' pistol, for example, is well made at a sensible price, and the Norica range also represents good value for money. Poor finish is often an indication of poor workmanship elsewhere. Some of the first airguns to be imported from China in the late 1970s were cheap but had little else to commend them. There are indications that this situation has since improved, but, if buying second-hand, beware.

Be particularly careful if buying a gun from any of the cheaper, less well-known ranges of airgun, because spares can often be difficult, if not impossible, to find. Fortunately, airguns have few moving parts and are generally reliable, but mainsprings and airseal washers will need replacement eventually, and availability of spares must be a consideration. In practice, a knowledgeable owner or gunsmith can often improvise, using a part adapted from another make of gun, but this is an unnecessary inconvenience.

Power

Since the advent of the first airgun magazines in the mid-'seventies and the resurgence of interest in airguns which these magazines have generated, the British airgun industry has undergone something of an upheaval. Some manufacturers have fallen victim to the recession, and have either gone out of business entirely or ceased the manufacture of airguns and concentrated on more viable aspects of their work. Those manufacturers remaining have found it necessary to produce new and better models to cope with the demand for high quality, high powered air rifles, which had previously only been available from the German companies. The competition has, as always, been good for the customer, and buyers are now very much spoilt for choice.

Webley and BSA have a useful range of airguns which have proved consistently popular over the years. Both manufacturers produce air rifles of good quality, with power near the legal limit of 12 foot pounds muzzle energy, as well as retaining the relatively low powered guns intended for youngsters. Webley's Vulcan and BSA's Airsporter and Mercury are well tried guns and have adequate power for hunting.

Perhaps I could take this opportunity to clarify one particular misconception among beginners to the sport of airgun shooting. Although adequate power is necessary when hunting, to ensure clean, humane kills, it is not always true that the most powerful gun is the best for the job. Consistent accuracy is a far more essential attribute in an airgun, and in fact airguns producing between about 7 and 12 foot pounds energy will cope effectively with small vermin at a sensible range.

Most manufacturers give an idea of the power of the airguns they are selling, and the monthly airgun magazines run regular tests on the most popular guns. It should not, therefore, prove too difficult to establish the relevant details on any gun which might be suitable for your requirements.

Calibre

Another question which will need to be considered when buying an airgun is the matter of calibre. A slightly tricky one, this, since even experts disagree as to which calibre is best for a particular application.

The choice, broadly, is between .177 and .22, that is .177 of an inch and .22 of an inch. Some pneumatics are available in .20 calibre, and some older weapons may have other calibres such as .25. However, for most practical purposes, .177 and .22 are the choices when buying an airgun, and it is these which we shall now consider.

The required calibre for serious competitive shooting is .177, and many clubs will insist upon this calibre for that reason. The small pellets have the advantage of travelling at relatively high velocity compared with the heavier .22, giving them a flatter trajectory and a good standard of accuracy. It is also worth remembering that they are less expensive – an important consideration to note, especially if the gun is to be used for plinking, which can be exceptionally heavy on pellets.

The .22 is traditionally the calibre for hunting with airguns, a tradition which has been fostered by manufacturers over the years. The theory behind their use for hunting is that they are more forceful than the .177, delivering more shock and thus more killing power. Some hunters, however, do prefer the flatter trajectory of the .177, feeling that the smaller pellet offers them the edge in accuracy. Against this, they must weigh the fact that the lighter pellet is a little more susceptible to being put off course by the wind in gusty weather conditions. At the end of the day, the decision must rest with the buyer.

I have hunted with many types of airgun in various calibres, and in my experience there is, generally, little difference between them. There are some situations, though, where the choice of calibre can make a difference. Grey squirrels are a pest in many woodland areas, and are fair game for the hunter. Ideally, with any vermin, a head shot is best, but I can remember, as a teenager, hunting these animals with a fairly powerful .177 air rifle, and my ability was perhaps a little less than ideal. I discovered that although a head shot would produce an instant, humane kill, an upper body shot was often ineffective, with follow up shots being necessary to despatch the animal. This I found disturbing, and close examination showed that the pellets had often passed right through the animals' bodies without imparting sufficient shock for an instant kill. Subsequent experience has shown that this situation is less likely to occur when .22 calibre is used (see Chapter 5 for further details).

Types of Airgun

Most of the makes of gun mentioned so far have one thing in common: they are spring powered. It is true to say that some are break-barrel types and others under-lever or side-lever, but the power comes from air which is forced out under pressure when a powerful steel spring gives up its energy as the trigger is released.

There are other types of airgun, however. Pump-up guns store a charge of air, which is then released at the pull of the trigger, either in a single rush or in a controlled series of bursts, giving several successive shots for each charge. The idea is not new, and has been utilised with varying degrees of success in many vintage airguns, although the use of modern materials for seals and valves has greatly improved the reliability and predictability of these weapons.

Many of the best known airguns in this group are made in the United States, but match shooters will know that Germany also produces high quality competition airguns using this system, and Spain and Japan have made examples of this type of gun, too.

A Milbro Cougar pistol showing break-barrel action.

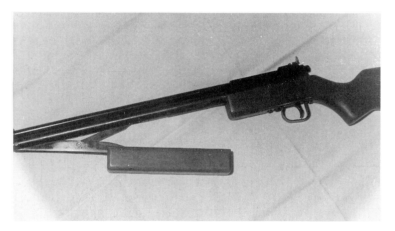

A pump up 'pneumatic' rifle, showing the pump in the open position.

The American Crosman, Sheridan and Daisy come most readily to mind in the field of pump-ups. Quality is very much related to price, with the cheaper ones being very poor indeed, and the more expensive examples often underrated. This is perhaps due to the dubious reputation some of the early American imports to Britain had as regards reliability. These guns were considered, rather undeservedly, as being all-powerful, and were credited with highly fanciful velocity figures in the days before instruments such as chronoscopes were available. Consequently, ambitious owners would pump them up well beyond recommended limits, destroying valves and seals in the process. Today, the law requires that safety release valves be built in so that legal muzzle energy figures cannot be exceeded, although high power versions are available for firearm certificate holders.

Advantages of pump-ups, or 'pneumatics' as they are sometimes called (strangely, since all airguns are technically pneumatics or 'air-powered' weapons), are that there is no recoil on discharge, and accuracy tends to be very good. These guns can also be left in a charged state for long periods without the worry of a spring to deteriorate – a great advantage when hunting.

On the negative side, pump-ups, depending upon type, often need up to half a dozen or more pumps to charge them, and this can be both noisy, if you are hunting, and exhausting, if you are plinking. Styling is often limited by the need to have a large pump lever incorporated into the design.

Apart from spring and pump airguns, there have come onto the market recently the results of some innovative ideas which have much to commend them. These ideas have been developed with the hunter in mind, but the guns concerned have also given a good account of themselves in field target competitions, and a great future is assured, provided that long-term reliability proves to be good. The indications are that, after a few initial 'hiccups', this will indeed be so.

The Theoben Sirocco utilises an inert gas to power the piston. The gas is permanently sealed in and is compressed on the cocking stroke. Like the pneumatics, the Sirocco may be left cocked and ready to fire for long periods without damage. This is useful when hunting, but is generally not a good idea from the safety viewpoint. The Sirocco is recoilless

The Webley Premier – an excellent second-hand buy.

and well made, and is consistent from shot to shot.

Saxby Palmer have come up with some very novel ideas, and have successfully introduced the air cartridge in a number of guns, starting with the now defunct Ensign Elite, and progressing through the Saturn and Galaxy rifles and the fascinating Orion 6 pistol. Development has been influenced by the military market, with the knowledge that a relatively inexpensive airgun, using a cartridge which could be made compatible with military calibres, could have attractions as a training medium.

These guns, produced in Stratford, utilise a pre-charged air cartridge that holds both the pellet and the charge of air which propels it. The advantages are obvious: no recoil, very quick reloading, and possible repeating facility depending upon the design of the individual weapon. These are not plinking weapons however, since charging the air cartridges is a little tedious if you are doing a lot of shooting at one time. Although rather expensive, the Saxby Palmer guns have much to commend them, and are sold complete with the necessary pump, which ideally needs to be permanently fixed in a convenient spot, such as in a garage or shed.

Imported CO_2 or gas powered weapons are occasionally offered for sale, but it should be understood that these guns require a firearm certificate in Britain, as do any air rifles which exceed the limit of 12 foot pounds muzzle energy (6 foot pounds in the case of air pistols). Gas operated weapons do, in fact, need a firearm certificate regardless of muzzle energy.

Incidentally, the Theoben Sirocco already mentioned does not fall into this category because the gas used is retained. It simply powers the piston, which then pushes the air before it and pushes the pellet out. So, it is still technically an air, rather than a gas, gun.

CHAPTER THREE

SOMEWHERE TO SHOOT

It will be apparent that there is little point in buying an airgun if you have nowhere suitable to use it, yet surprisingly many people do make this mistake, probably because they have a vague notion that 'any open space will do', having perhaps seen others out shooting. We have noted, however, that it is easy to break the law in this respect.

Plinking

In practice, most newcomers to the sport start in their own gardens or yards, and spend many happy hours firing away at improvised targets. Casual shooting at random or improvised targets is known as 'plinking', an American term which probably derived from the sound of a pellet striking a tin can, a much-used target with plinkers. Plinking is immensely popular and undemanding. It does not require the self-discipline of formal competitive target shooting, or the patient dedication of the hunter; in short, plinking is great fun. That is not to say that other forms of airgun shooting are not fun, just that plinking tends to be a little more relaxing.

Setting up a Backstop

There are just a few basic points to bear in mind when plinking in your own, or a friend's, garden. An adequate backstop or pellet trap should be set up behind the target area to catch and absorb the energy of spent pellets, and to prevent them from straying outside the boundaries of the garden. A backstop can be made from any appropriate materials, so long as it is large enough to catch the occasional 'flyer' (erratic shot). A few thicknesses of old carpet, or a large cardboard box stuffed tightly with newspapers laid flat, one on top of the other, will do an adequate job. Other good backstops are thick steel sheets, and even brick walls; but be warned, if a pellet strikes a hard surface at any angle other than a right angle, the resulting ricochet can cause a lot of damage. If you use steel or brick as a backstop, make sure you shoot at right angles to the target area. Avoid using bricks as a backstop if they present a facetted surface, as this, too, will deflect pellets.

The only time a backstop can be dispensed with is when you are hunting or shooting in large open spaces, but in these instances it is essential to ensure that nobody, and nothing breakable, is within range. Remember, a high powered air rifle is capable of ejecting its pellet at around 800 feet per second in .177 calibre, or around 600 feet per second in .22 calibre. A pellet can remain in flight for a couple of hundred yards or more and still retain enough of its energy at the end of its flight to cause damage or injury. Never underestimate the power of an airgun.

Types of Target

Part of the fun of shooting is in devising new and interesting types of target. Card targets are enjoyable enough, and enable you to gauge your performance by making specific score comparisons over a period of time. Targets which offer some sort of reaction when hit give a little more colour to the sport. Tin cans have always been popular, and make a satisfying noise when hit, but lower powered guns will cause pellets to bounce off steel cans, so be careful. This problem is unlikely to occur with soft drink or beer cans as these are now made from aluminium, which offers little resistance to even a low powered pellet.

Handymen may like to make a mobile type of target, such as one with hanging figures which jump when hit or one with resettable pegs. Steel is the best material to use, and should not be less than about 16 SWG thickness otherwise it will quickly distort and collect plenty of dents, if your airgun is reasonably powerful. Again, be careful to avoid ricochets.

It can be very enjoyable to shoot with other enthusiasts, and the competitive edge which this gives your shooting can greatly improve your standards of accuracy. Simple games are easy enough to devise, using all sorts of target, and scoring on a simple points system is usually appropriate, with the highest scorer being the winner.

Local Clubs

The ideal vehicle for competitive shooting is, of course, your local airgun club, which is next on the list of places where you can use an airgun legally. In recent years, many new clubs have sprung up all over Britain, offering friendly advice and practical help to new shooters. Ask your local airgun dealer for details of clubs in your own particular area, or study one of the excellent magazines which cater specifically for airgun users, as these frequently contain addresses of such clubs. Failing that, the police will often be able to advise you.

Clubs for airgun users vary widely in the emphasis they place on the various aspects of shooting with airguns. Some clubs are geared for indoor card target shooting, and may be keen on serious competitive shooting at national or even international level. Such clubs will usually insist on .177 calibre only, as this is the recognised calibre for formal target shooting.

Field target shooting clubs have become very popular, giving members the chance to fire all types of airgun in .177, .22, or even .20 calibre on an outdoor range at varying distances. This type of club offers excellent training for anyone who intends to hunt using an air weapon, and advice is always on hand for the newcomer. In my view, nobody should attempt to shoot at any living creature, vermin or not, unless they have first proved their consistent competence on a practice range – shooting at various distances, and under differing conditions and stances. Field target clubs offer just such experience.

Almost any type of air rifle or pistol is acceptable at most field target clubs, and you will have the opportunity of seeing and perhaps even trying out many varied weapons, including those which you would otherwise never have had a chance to try.

Starting your own Club

Assuming that there is no airgun club within practical distance from your home, you may like to think about the possibility of starting your own club. This is not a venture to be undertaken lightly. It could involve a good deal of work, but you may be fulfilling a need amongst many other enthusiasts in your area. The first step in forming any sort of club is to find other people with similar interests and enthusiasm, either by 'putting the word around' or by advertising in shop windows, or in the local newspaper. If you are ambitious enough, you may like to consider an article in one of the national airgun magazines, too.

The most difficult aspect of forming a new airgun club is finding a suitable venue. Great powers of tact and diplomacy will be required to persuade the appropriate individuals that you are a serious-minded enthusiast.

Pubs may have a room available for hire, provided you can convince the landlord that there is no chance whatever of ricochets, or damage to the room. Make sure that you take out appropriate insurance cover first though, and ensure that all your members are conversant with basic safety rules.

It is possible to make folding screens using plywood, with layers of thick carpeting and felt to absorb spent pellets, and these screens can be left on the premises ready to erect on club night. Pubs are popular venues in many parts of the country.

Army and territorial units sometimes have small indoor ranges which you may be able to rent on evenings when they are not in use, by contacting the local C.O. Quite a few shops are now installing ranges for the use of prospective customers; if you are on good terms with the owners, it may be possible to use their ranges when they are not required, provided the security of their premises is not jeopardised. Large garages or basement cellars can also be used as airgun ranges. There is no real shortage of potential sites for an indoor club.

Outdoor shooting for many, however, is what airgun shooting is all about, and if you can find an old quarry and can track down the owners you will have the ideal, safe venue for your field target shooting club.

Whatever premises you seek for your club, be prepared to pay for your shooting, and if you can obtain the security of a lease, so much the better. As a matter of courtesy, let the local police know about your club, and never be afraid to ask the advice of the police firearms officer regarding any legal aspects about which you may wish to know.

Your club, be it indoor or outdoor, will need to be organised along formal lines, with proper accounts for members to see on request. There should be a management committee to decide upon rules and general policy, to establish the standards of the club, and to oversee safety aspects. A chairperson should be nominated to control and direct periodic meetings, a secretary to keep the minutes of those meetings, and a treasurer to handle finances. These are the basic requirements for any such organisation.

Hunting Areas

You may prefer, however, to shoot alone, or in the company of just one or two friends. Perhaps, after plenty of practice in the garden, you see yourself as a hunter, trudging home after sunset, your air rifle over one shoulder and a plump, tasty rabbit over the other. Hunting is a subject which we shall explore in detail later in the book, but where to find a suitable hunting area is what we now have to consider.

It is fair to say that mainland Britain has a vast number of rabbits, wood pigeons, crows and rats, all of which are classed as vermin, and all of which are legitimate quarry for the airgun hunter. It is also fair to say that somebody else usually owns the land on which these creatures can be found, so your efforts must be directed:

(a) at finding the chosen quarry, and

(b) at gaining permission to shoot.

Should you turn up at a farm in scruffy jeans or camouflage gear, with your air rifle slung across your shoulder like some Mexican bandit, then ask permission to shoot, it is most unlikely you will be successful. Put yourself in the landowner's shoes, and imagine a stranger confronting you with a request to wander through your land, past your cows and sheep, shooting at vermin with a powerful air rifle, and ask yourself what *your* answer would be!

The best way of securing a shoot, as this type of hunting venue is termed, is to ask someone who knows you quite well if you can shoot over his or her land. If you do not know any landowners yourself, arrange for some friends or colleagues to introduce you to a landowner of their acquaintance.

Failing this, there is nothing to stop you knocking on doors and asking permission, but *do* dress respectably, and be polite, even if permission to shoot is refused. Do not expect something for nothing; always offer to pay for your shooting, or to help around the farm. This may well swing the chances in your favour. Above all, make it clear by your attitude and actions that you are a responsible sort of person who will respect and observe the Countryside Code, and who will have due regard to safety and concern for other people's property. Experience has shown that shooting rights are more likely to be obtained by an individual request rather than by two or three airgunners approaching a landowner together.

Point out the positive aspects of your sport. Arable farms are often plagued by wood pigeons, particularly during the winter months when food is scarce, and an offer to thin these out, occasionally, may be well received by a busy farmer who has little time to hunt vermin himself. Rabbits, as well as pigeons, can be a very worrying threat to crops which are particularly vulnerable at certain stages of their development, and a determined and responsible attempt to reduce the rabbit population may again be welcomed.

Apart from farmers, there are a number of organisations, such as local authorities, government departments and private firms, which often have overgrown tracts of land, surplus to immediate requirements. These areas of land may be unfenced, and unofficially used by unauthorised shooters already. In these cases, a written request should be made, preferably typewritten and stating your specific requirements and exact intentions regarding the use of the land, i.e. frequency of intended use, type of quarry, and any payment which you are prepared to offer. Your letter should be addressed to the head of the organisation concerned and, if possible, you should also enclose a copy of a plan detailing the area over which you hope to be allowed to shoot.

If you meet with success in your efforts, the acceptance letter should be photocopied, and the copy carried around with you when you shoot, as evidence of your right to be there. The owners might well welcome the chance of having an unofficial warden on their land, and may request that you report trespassers. Any conditions laid down by the organisation must be strictly observed, and avoid leaving litter or disturbing wild creatures which are not officially classed as vermin.

Finally, if all else fails, you can, like many readers of the national airgun magazines, advertise your requirements in the hope that some farmer will take pity on you and offer you a shoot. In fact, a small number of enterprising farmers already advertise their own facilities to hunters. If you have the money and are prepared to travel, you are more or less assured of a shoot somewhere in the country.

CHAPTER FOUR
USING THE GUN

Zeroing the Sights

Having bought your gun, it will be necessary to zero the sights, regardless of whether you intend to use the standard, or 'open', sights or a telescopic sight.

The idea of zeroing is simply to ensure that the sights of the gun are correctly lined up. This will ensure that the gun is capable of hitting the target accurately at the distance at which you intend to shoot.

Start by ensuring that the gun is in good condition, with no loose screws or bolts. Ensure there is no excessive play in pivot pins, and check that the sights are securely fitted and cannot vibrate loose. It is particularly important when using a telescopic sight ('scope), which may work loose if not securely fixed with good quality mounts. In the event of severe 'scope creep, if an arrestor block is not available, a little thin paper smeared with impact adhesive will often provide a cure, as long as the mounts are tightened onto the paper first, rather than directly to the gun.

The method of adjustment may be by set screws, ramp, or a knurled wheel or similar arrangement, and there will be adjustment for elevation (up and down) and windage (side to side). Adjustment is carried out on the rearsight only, with the foresight almost always being fixed, though on some guns a degree of elevation may be provided on the foresight.

Set up card targets, using a suitable backstop, at the distance at which you expect to do much of your shooting, then take time to establish a comfortable firing point. Bales of hay or cushions are best to enable you to achieve a rock-steady, rested firing position. Do *not* lean the gun on the rest when firing, but hold it in a comfortable firing position and use the rest simply to prevent movement as you fire. Keep pellets handy so that you do not need to alter your position while firing.

Open sights When sighting with open sights, the forsight blade or bead should be central in the rearsight V or aperture, depending which is fitted. The top of the foresight should appear flush with the top of the rearsight notch, or central if an aperture rearsight is fitted. Obviously, if a 'scope is fitted, it is a simple matter of lining up cross hairs, or hairs and post, or whatever set up the 'scope uses.

Fig. 1 Sighting:

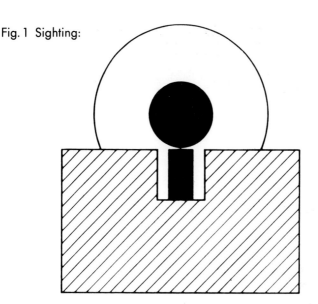

**The foresight blade should be centred in the blade
of the rearsight and flush with the top of it**

Fig. 2 Zeroing:

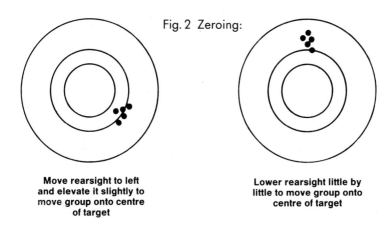

**Move rearsight to left
and elevate it slightly to
move group onto centre
of target**

**Lower rearsight little by
little to move group onto
centre of target**

With open sights it is a good idea to keep a small area of white target above the sights, lining up just below the bull instead of spot on. This makes for better consistency, in that the black sights do not show up well against the black centre of the target.

The trigger should be gently squeezed, avoiding any tendency to pull or jerk. Each shot should be aimed at *exactly* the same spot, regardless of where the pellets go, and four or five shots should be fired at the target before any move is made to go and look at the result, assuming that the pellets are at least hitting the card of course.

If your shooting has been steady and the gun is in good condition, you should find that all the shots you have fired are clustered in a fairly tight group somewhere on the target card. If they happen to be in the bull, there is no need to read on, since the gun is shooting spot on and obviously suits your own eyesight and method of shooting. You can congratulate yourself on your prowess, too.

However, if, as is more likely, the holes are all in one corner or other of the target, then some adjustment will be necessary.

Ignore any 'fliers', and simply take note of the trend of the pattern of pellet holes. To raise the pattern of hits, assuming that they are falling low, simply raise the rearsight a little at a time, firing a further four or five shots each time until the pattern is level with the centre of the target. Obviously if the shots are going high it will be necessary to lower the rearsight.

To move the point of impact to the left, adjust the rearsight to the left, and vice-versa if the shots need to fall further to the right.

To sum up then, move the point of impact *up* by *raising* the rearsight. Move the point of impact to one side by moving the rearsight in the direction you want the shots to go.

The important point with zeroing is not to be in too much of a hurry but to allow your shooting to be as consistent as possible, otherwise you could find yourself doing the job all over again as your technique improves. Try to obtain as much target practice as possible, but avoid shooting when you are tired, as your performance will fall off noticeably.

Common Faults

As with most sports, bad habits picked up early on can take a long time to eliminate, but having said that, be sure that what you are trying to correct really is a bad habit and not just an individual way of shooting – the two are not necessarily the same, and many experts in various sports have their own particular technique which works well for them.

The classic fault among shooters, including many who should know better, is *trigger snatching*. The results of this fault, and it really is a fault, are inconsistency from shot to shot, and a predominance of 'fliers' (erratic shots) is inevitable. Snatching is caused by impatience and giving insufficient thought to the shot. If your gun has an adjustable trigger, it will be possible to reduce the weight at which the trigger lets off, and this will help to reduce the tendency to snatch. Don't overdo it though, or the airgun could become unstable and fire unexpectedly, with possible dangerous consequences. A competent dealer will be happy to carry out the job for you, if you prefer.

The trigger should be gently squeezed, with a smooth, steady movement. There should be no attempt to anticipate the point at which the gun actually fires, because that is indicative of the second commonest shooting fault, flinching.

Flinching is common among newcomers to firearm or shotgun shooting. Nervousness or anticipation of the explosion of the shot, albeit a small one, when the gun fires causes a jerky motion as the trigger is released.

Airguns are, of course, much less noisy than firearms, yet flinching is nevertheless still common among airgun shooters. Fortunately, this fault is usually eliminated as the shooter gains familiarity and confidence with the weapon.

A good marksman develops a rhythm to his shooting, so that even his breathing does not influence the quality of his shots. He knows that the wavering of the gun when it is being lined up on the target is actually quite normal, and can never be totally eliminated, only controlled. Beginners are often alarmed by the fact that the gun barrel seems to have a mind of its own, and trembles uncontrollably, but in fact the art is in accepting this to a degree, and then knowing at which point to release the trigger.

Allow your shooting to be governed by a fixed series of movements. Cock and load the gun, release the safety catch if one is fitted, raise the gun to a point above the target, then lower it to just below the centre of the target. Finally, edge the sights up a fraction until the bullseye is lined up with just a narrow band of white below it, if you are using a conventional target card.

By the time you reach the point at which the shot is released, you should have already begun to squeeze the trigger very gently. Constant practice and familiarity with the gun will enable you to coincide the release of the trigger with the lining up of the sights on the appropriate point on the target, without snatching or otherwise spoiling the shot.

Holding the sights A common fault among airgun users, particularly beginners, is to attempt to hold the sights on target for too long. If the shot is not fired fairly soon after coming on target, the weight of the gun will cause it to waver, as will the natural effect of breathing, and accuracy will be lost. Arrange your preliminary actions so that you are gently exhaling as the sights are lined up for the shot, but if you are unable to take the shot reasonably quickly, lower the gun for a moment or two and then start again, when the breathing rhythm has steadied.

The quality of shooting will obviously be impaired if attempts are made to shoot immediately after an arduous walk or climb. The body needs time to recover, to settle heartbeat, breathing and tired muscles, and these factors are vital to consider when hunting, because it is tempting to take a shot at a rabbit, for instance, which you have laboriously stalked for the last hour, as soon as you are at a point which affords a clear, in-range shot. You owe it to the rabbit, if not to yourself, to prepare yourself properly for the shot, particularly as you are likely to be contending with other problems, such as thistles, sharp rocks, and possibly pouring rain.

I have already stressed the need for safety at all times when using an airgun. Always be aware of your surroundings, watching out in particular for small children, who have little understanding of danger. Remember, the responsibility rests with the one using the gun, regardless of how stupid or inconsiderate the actions of others may prove to be.

Pistols

Most newcomers to airguns start with an air rifle, wheareas in my own case I started with an air pistol. Perhaps for this reason I have always had a particular interest in pistols, and have quite a large collection of them. I feel, too, that they offer a greater challenge, being more difficult to shoot well than a rifle, and anyone persevering with an air pistol will gain considerable satisfaction when they develop the necessary skill.

The basic techniques already described also apply in large measure to air pistols as well as to rifles. The only real difference is that the pistol is not so well supported as the rifle, and the task is to work at providing steady support for the shooting arm.

Constant shooting, especially with a fairly heavy pistol, will eventually strengthen the arm and wrist muscles, giving improved control. Matchmen shoot with one hand only, keeping the other hand out of the way by putting it in a pocket, or hooking the thumb into the waistband of the trousers. If you intend doing any match shooting your technique will need to be similar to this.

Those whose lives depend on the fast, accurate use of pistols employ

This pistol can be adapted to a rifle by the addition of a simple clip-on stock.

The correct way to use a pistol – note the shooting hand is extended.

the two-handed technique, with the non-shooting hand supporting the hand holding the pistol and, in practice, this can give a steady aim and a correspondingly high standard of accuracy.

A pistol should be treated as an extension of the hand, and sighting can be visualised as the action of pointing a finger. In fact, many successful pistol marksmen shoot almost instinctively, rather than depending solely upon the sights, and there are many stories about some marksmen removing the sights of their pistols completely and still turning in scores which would embarrass most of us.

If you are using open sights against a dark target you may find that they do not stand out too well. This problem can be overcome by putting a small amount of typewriter correction fluid over the upper edges of the sights. The material rubs off reasonably easily if you feel the need to remove it at a later date.

CHAPTER FIVE

UNDERSTANDING BALLISTICS

Ballistics is a rather frightening word, which conjures up a picture of serious faced, white coated scientists employed by the Ministry of Defence, huddling over complicated testing equipment, or perhaps police pathologists studying a bullet taken from the body of a murder victim in an effort to establish which gun, or type of gun, fired the fatal shot.

In fact, ballistics is simply the term used to describe the study of the behaviour of any type of projectile in flight, be it a stone, bullet, or even a guided missile. From the airgunner's point of view it is the study of how pellets behave once they have been fired. It may sound unnecessarily technical, but it is, nevertheless, important for the shooter to have at least a basic understanding of what an airgun pellet is doing on its flight from the barrel to the target. Such a knowledge will enable him to gauge the likely behaviour of the pellet under a given set of circumstances.

Smooth and Rifled Barrels

Most modern air weapons, except the very cheapest examples, have rifled barrels rather than smooth bores. That is to say, the interior of the barrel is machined to leave shallow grooves in a gradual spiral pattern for the whole length of the barrel. These grooves grip the pellet as it is

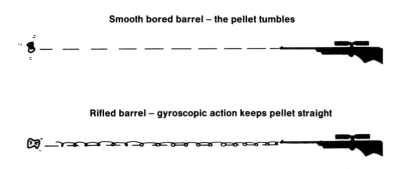

Fig. 3 Effect of smooth and rifled barrels.

propelled through the barrel by the charge of air behind it, and the pellet emerges from the muzzle rotating on its axis. Gunsmiths and the military discovered many years ago that imparting such a spin to a projectile causes it to travel with greater accuracy and consistency on its path to the target. Rifling also enabled streamlined projectiles to be used, which are less likely to be affected by wind resistance than spherical missiles, and are thus more efficient over a longer range. Fired from a smooth barrel, a bullet-shaped projectile will gradually tumble in flight, allowing wind forces to act upon a greater surface area and deflect the projectile from its intended path. The principles of rifling were discovered as early as the sixteenth century, but were not really developed until much later. It was not until breech loading came into being that the full potential of rifled barrels could be realised. With the old muzzle loaders, loading was difficult and tedious, and likely to be dangerous if a rifled barrel was fitted. In such a case the projectile had to be forced past the rifling grooves before it was seated and ready for firing. Consequently, the traditional smooth-bored muskets remained popular until breech loading overcame the problems associated with rifling.

The effect of rifling on the flight of the pellet may be clearly seen by comparing pellets fired at a hard steel surface, first from an airgun with a rifled barrel, and then from a smooth bored airgun. At close range, the front of the pellet will be dented in each case, to a greater or lesser degree, depending upon the velocity of the guns used. Shoot from a greater distance away from the target, though, and then compare pellets. The rifled barrel weapon will continue to produce pellets which are dented at the front, but the pellets fired by the smooth-bore gun will be dented on the front, sides or back; in fact anywhere.

The reason for the difference is that rifling induces a gyroscopic action in the pellet, which makes it resistant to the forces of the air acting upon it. A pellet from a smooth-bore gun, however, gradually turns in the air as it is propelled along by its charge of air. As it turns the air catches at the uneven surfaces, unless it is a perfect sphere, and flips it in several directions. This accounts for the relative inaccuracy of smooth-bored guns. Obviously, the higher the velocity of the gun, the greater the eventual margin of error is likely to be when the pellet eventually strikes its target. The higher velocity will have a correspondingly greater effect on the pellet as it begins to tumble.

Manufacturers are able to get away with installing smooth-bore barrels in lower priced airguns because, owing to the lower power of the cheaper guns and the correspondingly shorter effective range, the reduced accuracy is less apparent than in a more powerful gun. Smooth-bores can be simple brass-lined tubes, whereas a steel rifled barrel must be carefully machined using special equipment. A rifled barrel is, therefore, more expensive to produce. As a youngster I shot with a smooth-bored Diana air rifle, and was able to shoot with consistent accuracy, but only at ranges of up to 7 or 8 metres. This range is perhaps acceptable for a youngster, but not for an experienced shooter.

Trajectory of the Pellet

Gravity is another force which acts upon projectiles in flight, as well as air turbulence and general wind resistance. The effects of all these forces can be best illustrated by throwing stones. A large, heavy stone requires a considerable amount of energy to propel it. Its passage can be seen as a fairly steep curve – the stone travels in an arc as it leaves your hand. To overcome the weight of the stone and the effect of gravity, it is necessary for you to propel it at a very steep angle, and it returns to the ground at a similar angle. Throw it into a high wind and it is unlikely to travel as far as if you had thrown it *with* the wind.

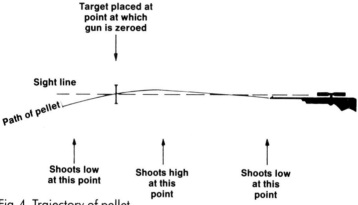

Fig. 4 Trajectory of pellet.

Launch a lighter stone and you will discover that it can be thrown at a shallower angle than the large stone to reach the same distance for a given expenditure of energy. It then also returns to the ground at a similar shallow angle, or trajectory. Throw the lighter stone into the wind and it *may* be less affected than its larger brother because it has less surface area on which the air can act. On the other hand, its lighter weight makes it easier for the wind to act upon it in flight, influencing the flight path which it takes through the air.

Relating this example to the question of which calibre to use – does the lighter, smaller pellet travel faster and, therefore, further for a given amount of energy than the larger pellet? Will it not also travel in a flatter trajectory, instead of curving steeply as it travels? Will this fact make it a more accurate and generally better calibre to use?

The answers, unfortunately, are not entirely straightforward. The trajectory curve – the flight of a small, light pellet like a .177 through the air on its way to the target — will be shallow, more of a straight line than the pronounced curve of the trajectory of a heavier, larger pellet like a .22 or .25, and consequently the allowance needed on elevation (up and down adjustment) for long range shots is less for the smaller, lighter pellet. A gun zeroed at 20 metres may well still be almost spot on at 10 or even 20 metres more, whereas the use of a larger calibre will necessitate adjusting the point of aim by several centimetres for the same range variation. In a sense it may be said that the .177 is more accurate than a larger calibre.

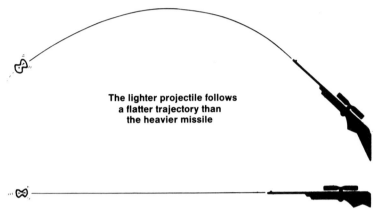

**The lighter projectile follows
a flatter trajectory than
the heavier missile**

Fig. 5 Comparison between light and heavy missile trajectories.

Some would argue that because a small calibre pellet can travel very fast, needing relatively little energy to propel it, it may be less prone to being knocked off line by side winds than a heavier pellet. Proponents of the heavier calibres might correspondingly suggest that the weight of the slower moving heavier pellet makes it less of a pushover for any passing breeze. There is actually relatively little solid reliable scientific evidence available regarding airgun ballistics. The much lower velocities than those attained by firearms mean that data obtained from firearm testing is not necessarily applicable to airguns. Experience has in fact shown this to be the case, though obviously some aspects will be the same. Perhaps the reason for a shortage of firm data relating to airgun ballistics is that there are many factors involved, each capable of affecting one or more of the others. The effects of rifling have already been mentioned. Small variations in individual rifle barrels, even on the same make and model gun, can make a difference, as can variations in pellet type, effects of rifling on the pellet, damage to the pellet itself, etc.

My own experience, which has not really been very scientific, is that the lighter .177 calibre is inclined to be more affected by sidewinds than the .22, but this is the result of casual observation using a relatively limited number of weapons. The results may well be very different if a wider range of airguns is used, and tests carried out at various distances, using different makes of airgun, firing different configurations and weights of pellet: remember that pellets can vary in weight depending upon type. Accuracy and performance can be influenced by the considerable weight variation between individual pellets of identical type and calibre within the same batch. You will see that the task of carrying out objective, meaningful testing is not as straightforward as it might at first appear.

Pellet/Airgun Combination

It might be assumed that .177 is more desirable as a calibre than .22 by virtue of the fact that the pellet travels faster, and is, therefore, more likely to be effective in penetrating the target, than the larger calibre. This assumption only tells a part of the story though, because the speed of the pellet is just one of several factors involved in the effectiveness of that pellet as a vermin killer. The weight of the pellet is another factor, as we have seen by comparing the performance of thrown stones of different sizes. The actual type, or configuration of the pellet is also important.

With regard to the effectiveness of a pellet/airgun combination when shooting live vermin – and it is very relevant to match a particular airgun to a pellet which has been proved to suit it – the vital point is to give consideration to what exactly it is that kills the animal. This may seem an irrelevant statement at first; after all, it is the pellet which kills the animal. That is true, but does the animal die of loss of blood, damage to vital organs, shock, fright, or a combination of these things?

When a pellet leaves the barrel of an airgun, it carries a certain 'charge' of energy. This charge of energy is related to the velocity at which the pellet is propelled by the charge of air behind it, and also to the weight of the pellet itself. The energy is imparted from energy stored in the coiled spring (assuming a spring air weapon is being used) and released when the trigger is pulled. As the pellet travels on the path from the muzzle of the gun, this initial 'muzzle energy' (which as we have already seen is limited to 12 foot pounds for an air rifle, and 6 foot pounds for a pistol) gradually reduces as the pellet speeds towards the target. Wind resistance, gravity, air turbulence, pellet weight and shape all have an effect upon the trajectory. By the time the pellet reaches the target, for example, a rabbit, the energy 'stored' in the pellet may be down to, say, 6 foot pounds from an initial muzzle energy of 11 or 12 foot pounds, depending upon range and other factors. As the pellet strikes the rabbit, some or all of that residual energy is given up into the body of the animal.

Let us assume that a high velocity .177 or even .22 air rifle is fired at a rabbit at, for instance, 20 metres. The hunter is a beginner who does not feel confident enough in his ability to take a head shot, so he aims at the upper body of the rabbit, which presents a much larger, easier target. The pellet strikes the chest area of the animal, passing through skin first, then flesh, and finally, missing the bones of the rib cage, the pellet speeds on, giving up part of its energy as it does so, through resistance of the body tissues. The pellet misses the heart and other vital organs although there is localised tissue damage, and then passes out of the other side of the chest of the rabbit to expend the remainder of its energy in a rocky bank or other obstacle behind the animal.

The rabbit leaps high into the air as it is hit, then runs, apparently unharmed, for thirty or forty metres before disappearing into cover. The hunter thinks he has missed the rabbit, as it does not appear to be damaged in any way. He may leave the area to search for another, and the same thing may well happen again. If he should study the ground where the animal was hit, he may discover droplets of blood but more likely there will be no indications of a successful hit at all; any bleeding usually tends to be internal, in view of the small size of an airgun pellet. The hunter may be no wiser even after careful scrutiny of the area where the rabbit was shot. The rabbit may possibly survive if the wound is fairly clean, but is more likely to die a slow, lingering death over a period of hours, or even days.

The above scenario is not fanciful fiction, but is based upon actual experience and observation. Consider now another example.

A hunter with a slightly lower powered air rifle, in .22 calibre, takes a shot at a rabbit from 20 metres, and hits it in the chest. The pellet strikes the bones of the rib cage and breaks one of the ribs, fragments of which tear through the lung area, causing severe internal bleeding and impairing the animal's breathing. The energy of the pellet has been fairly well expended by striking the bone, and it continues to travel more slowly, and in a different direction, because it has been deflected by the bone. It finally comes to rest inside the chest cavity, just below the heart; all its energy has been expended inside the animal. When the pellet hits the bone, fragments (being of soft lead) may fly off the main part of the pellet and tear through soft tissue before their energy, too, is used up. The nervous system of the animal suffers a severe shock as a result of the energy transfer from the pellet. This, coupled with sudden, severe loss of blood from vital areas torn by fragments of pellet and bone, causes a quick death.

Often, with this last type of hit, the rabbit may leap into the air and start to run. It may even reach cover, but dies very quickly. I have read of game animals in Africa being shot and then running for a quarter of a mile before collapsing in death. Perhaps nervous energy propels the muscles even as death occurs. However, whatever the reason, one point is clear – always go for a head shot when shooting live animals, or risk losing the animal and, worse, causing it to suffer.

Apart from the obvious value of head shots when shooting vermin, there are a number of lessons to be learned from the two examples detailed above. It will be clear that a larger pellet has more chance of hitting something important as it strikes the target. The higher the velocity, the better the chance of a pellet passing right through the animal without giving up all of its energy inside the animal's body. This point is likely to be academic anyway if the pellet, regardless of velocity, strikes a vital organ, since death is then more or less assured. A larger pellet entering the body of an animal must have a greater effect on the nervous system than a smaller pellet, and will impart a correspondingly greater degree of shock, and so improve the chances of a quicker kill.

It is, for instance, quite possible to kill a small animal or bird by hitting it with a projectile which does not even penetrate the body. Marbles or ball bearings fired from catapults come to mind here, and the shock of being struck by a large, albeit quite slow moving projectile is often sufficient to kill quickly, without any penetration of the body, and often without even severe tissue or bone damage.

The reason is that the large missile represents a substantial amount of energy. On impact, this energy is given up into the body of the target animal, imparting a massive, potentially lethal shock to the nervous system. Even without other damage, shock can and does kill. It is also one of the greatest killers of people, and is one of the reasons why accident victims are encouraged by the emergency services to go to hospital for a check up even if they have no obvious injury.

Evidence of the effects of shock have been known to the military and to firearm users for many years. Certain modern weapons in current use fire a small bullet at a very high velocity. The shape of the bullet is such that it tumbles on impact, causing a severe wound and associated shock, and can kill, even when a non-vital area is hit. The old wild west cowboys knew that the big .45 calibre bullet travelled relatively slowly, and had a short range when fired from a handgun, but it was a sure man-killer. High velocity small calibres could not be relied upon to do the same job.

Pellet Construction

Pellet construction has a part to play in successful, clean kills, too. Some types of pellet are solid and heavy for their size. Their weight makes them formidable when they impact, expending their energy, and they are inclined to tumble when they hit, creating a severe wound channel and imparting a high level of shock. They stay in one piece as they strike and do not fragment, and any damage is limited to that done by the main pellet itself.

Some non-lead pellets do not flatten on impact, and consequently penetrate better. This can be an advantage, as the further the pellet travels, the more likely it is to hit something important. On the other

Different pellet configurations. From left to right – pointed, roundheaded, prometheus, sabot and wadcutter.

hand, it may travel right through without giving up enough of its energy to kill, though this type does tend to tumble on impact, and then stop quite quickly.

Almost as a contradiction to our tests with the stones, some light alloy pellets are so light that they lose momentum too quickly to be effective at long ranges. A degree of compromise is obviously called for when selecting a suitable pellet.

Soft lead pellets have advantages and disadvantages. If you like to eat the rabbits you shoot, the presence of lead fragments in the meat is unlikely to help your digestion, and can cause lead poisoning. From the point of view of the hunter though, the traditional lead diabolo shaped pellets do quite an efficient job.

Diabolo pellets travel through the air very well and are fairly light for their size, giving a straighter trajectory and consequently good accuracy. They deform very easily when they strike bone, and a misshapen pellet causes more tissue damage than a perfectly formed one. Even if they do not become deformed they often tumble on impact, giving a similar effect. Soft lead pellets also fly apart if the velocity is high enough and the bone sufficiently hard, and this can do considerable damage. In practice, small animals and birds have fairly fragile bones which offer no real resistance but they do their part in absorbing the energy from the pellet well enough and a firm shock to the nervous system of the animal is ensured.

The diabolo pellet has certainly stood the test of time, and still outperforms just about every other pellet configuration in its various guises. The shape of the diabolo is not perfect from the aerodynamic point of view, but it has two points of contact with the rifling (more in some newer designs) which reduces friction compared with pellets or bullets that have continuous multiple contact with the rifling. The cutaway design of the diabolo reduces weight, increasing velocity, size for size.

Perhaps the best design, albeit probably one which is difficult to manufacture, would be an aerodynamic bullet shape, with a 'boat' tail to reduce drag. It would have two shallow driving bands to grip the rifling, one at the front, the other at the rear. These would be soft, so that they would flatten by the time the pellet left the barrel to avoid upsetting the aerodynamics of the projectile more than absolutely necessary. Lastly, the pellet would be hollow, so that on impact it would deform considerably, causing greater tissue damage and consequent shock to the quarry. Being hollow, the velocity would be good, and all the energy would be transferred to the target by the pellet's deformation when it hits the target. Perhaps some form of weakness lines could be built into the pellet without affecting aerodynamic principles. Such lines could allow the pellet to mushroom more effectively on impact. The principle of hollow point bullets, which mushroom on impact, causing a massive shock wound, is already established in the firearms field. Although hollow point airgun pellets are available, there is scant evidence to indicate that they expand any more than a standard pellet at a given velocity. There is nothing wrong with the principle, but since soft, hollow lead pellets spread on impact anyway, it is hard to see any benefit from using hollow pointed pellets unless, as I have suggested, pellets could be made with built-in weakness lines, without adversely affecting their performance in flight. Whereas a loss of velocity of, say, a hundred feet per second in a firearm would not be noticed, a similar loss in a projectile from an airgun could not be tolerated.

It will be seen, then, that the matter of ballistics holds as many questions as answers. Surely, though, this is part of the great attraction of airgun shooting, as we seek constantly after improvements, learning from our disappointments and building on our successes.

CHAPTER SIX

COMPETITIVE AIRGUN SHOOTING

Having shot your air rifle or pistol on your own for some time you may well become curious to know how well your shooting compares with that of other airgun enthusiasts. Many people start to take a step towards competitive shooting by inviting a friend around for a plinking session. It is inevitable that you will compare scores, finding out who is able to knock over the most tin cans, hit the bullseye on a card target the most times, or turn in the highest score over half a dozen target cards.

If your performance is good and you consistently shoot high scores, then it is only natural you will want to compete against a much wider field. The answer is to join your local club and make a note of all competitions which are coming up. There are open competitions advertised from time to time, and you may prefer to shoot in one of these before deciding whether to join a club. An open competition is simply a shooting match in which the entries are not restricted to club members only, as many matches inevitably are.

Open Competitions

To compete in an open competition just read the published rules, or send for full details, enclosing a stamped addressed envelope for the reply. Usually competitors can turn up on the day and shoot, but sometimes it is necessary to obtain an entrance form, pay a fee in advance, and shoot at a specified time.

If field target shooting is of interest to you, there is a separate chapter devoted specifically to this branch of the sport. This chapter covers general aspects of competitive shooting, and is intended to let you know what is available to those who have an interest in competitive shooting.

Bell Target Shooting

Should you happen to live in the Midlands, you have probably already heard of bell target shooting. Sometimes referred to as the 'pints and pellets' or 'pellets and pints' sport, bell target shooting is a well established sport which has been in existence for more than a hundred years. It reached a peak during the years between the First and Second

World Wars. It suffered something of a decline after the Second World War but has regained popularity in recent years, together with the resurgence of interest in airguns generally.

Bell target shooting has traditionally been associated with pubs and working men's clubs, where the sport has always been taken very seriously, with leagues being established alongside the local darts or snooker league, and clubs travelling back and forth to compete against one another. There is a certain appeal in shooting at a target that makes a noise (hence the popularity of the ubiquitous tin can), and bell target shooting appeals audibly as well as socially. There is no doubt that this is indeed a social sport, and many clubs have traditionally vied with one another to attract the best marksmen. A good bell target shooter is not necessarily the best marksman though. In the boisterous atmosphere of a pub or club, with comments being bandied back and forth, glasses rattling, people shouting, and smoke wafting across the target area, it can be very difficult to concentrate fully upon shooting well. As a consequence, the successful bell target shooter is probably someone who shoots well, but can also handle the rowdy atmosphere and remain unaffected. Very much a team sport, bell target shooting is for those who enjoy a lively social aspect to their sport. Round or pointed pellets are used at 6 yards in two series of 10 shots in 15 minutes, with two sighting shots before each series and a 20-minute interval.

Running Boar Shooting

A type of shooting known as running boar shooting was introduced at the 1972 Olympic Games in Munich as a small-bore rifle shooting event. It was not long before the sport was adapted to suit airguns.

The original running boar shoots were 50 metre events for firearms but the adapted version utilises .177 calibre 'scoped air rifles, shooting at a range of 10 metres. The target is a picture of a European wild boar and has concentric target circles marked on it. It is motor driven to cross a two metre opening in five seconds, or two and a half seconds. The targets come in pairs, one facing the left and the other facing to the right. This type of shooting is not unlike snap shooting in that there is a limited amount of time allowed (or available) for the actual shot.

Some clubs buy the running boar ranges ready built, and there are a number of different designs available at various costs. Some enterprising clubs build their own running boar systems and, provided they satisfy the required standard of operation, these serve perfectly well, and allow many shooters to sample running boar shooting who would not otherwise have the opportunity to do so. This type of shooting is reminiscent of fairground shooting of ducks and ping pong balls, so it tends to capture people's imaginations. It has even been featured on television, which is usually the hallmark of a fairly wide acceptance of a sport.

10 metre and 6 yard Target Shooting

Established indoor target shooting, apart from the bell target shooting already mentioned, is available as two distinct disciplines. These are 10 metre and 6 yard target shooting. You will find clubs offering both types of shooting, but some clubs specialise, so if you have any particular preference it is worth checking beforehand.

You will be required to use only .177 calibre for either discipline. A recoilless rifle (or pistol) will eventually prove to be a necessity if you are really serious about competitive target shooting, since only these guns have the consistency to produce regular high scores. That is not to say that other types of airgun are not effective, merely that we are talking in terms of millimetre accuracy, and any slight edge which a better gun may give you needs to be seized upon, if you are to make an impact upon the competitive target scene. For this reason, it may be wise not to buy a gun immediately upon joining a club, as a club gun is often available, or you may be able to borrow one. Naturally, a recoilless airgun of top quality is not cheap, and it is, therefore, important to be absolutely sure that target shooting of this type is definitely for you before laying out large sums of money on equipment.

10 metre target shooting is a little more demanding than 6 yard target shooting because of the greater range involved, though it may seem to be a relatively insignificant difference at first glance. What this means in practice is that scores tend, on average, to be a little lower for 10 metre target work than 6 yard, since any aiming errors that exist are magnified over the greater distance. Even more care is, therefore, needed at this range, with particular attention being paid to breathing, rhythm, firing stance, and other factors.

In 10 metre shooting, scoring is by a method known as inward gauging. The higher score counts if the pellet has broken a line on the target card. The card itself carries one or five individual targets of black on white, and a full match course at 10 metres is of unlimited sighting shots, with 40 or 60 shots to be counted. A time limit is imposed, and the course of shots must be fitted into one and a half hours for Ladies and Juniors, and two and a quarter hours for Men. Local variations exist.

6 yard target shooting follows similar lines to the 10 metre discipline, except that the target cards differ and take account of the shorter range.

Match rifles use dioptre sights, with interchangeable foresight ring and variable rear aperture. Pistols use open sights.

Postal Competitions

Finally, if you are not too keen on travelling all over the country to shoot competitively, postal competitions are popular. Many clubs participate in these, and they give airgun users the opportunity of competing in nationally organised events without stepping outside their own club, except perhaps to compete in the finals, once the preliminary results are made known.

Authenticated and witnessed target cards are sent off to the adjudicating body which has organised the postal competition. The results are then collated and competitors graded according to results, so that they are able to compete with others of similar aptitude.

Organisers of postal competitions usually insist that target cards are sent in 'as shot', without having been gauged first. Other rules relevant to this type of contest are supplied to the individual on receipt of the entry form, together with any fee which may be payable.

Trigger Pressure

When it comes to target shooting on a competitive basis, there are rules and regulations relating to the guns and other equipment to which you need to adhere, and full details of these are provided by the organisers of each competition and should be studied in depth. If you are a pistol enthusiast and intend competing at either 6 yards or 10 metres, you will need to ensure that the weight at which the trigger of your pistol releases is not less than 500 grams. The better quality pistols have finely adjustable triggers, and a light trigger helps to reduce excessive movement of the pistol when firing. This is an advantage, provided it is not below the specified minimum. A very light trigger can be dangerous and, in addition, if you have been practising using an ultra light trigger setting then you will have become accustomed to shooting at that setting. Should you enter a competition and have the pistol checked, you will be asked to adjust the trigger to the specified weight. You may then be likely to find that your scores suffer because you are unused to the new trigger weight. Other checks include maximum weight – 5 kg for rifles, 1.5 kg for pistols – and dimensions.

The trigger let off pressure can be gauged by the use of an accurate spring balance with the appropriate metric calibration. The test should be carried out with great care to ensure safety. Cheap pistols are not generally provided with an adjustable trigger and the standard weight is likely to be well above the 500 grams limit, unless the pistol has been modified by a specialist or by the owner.

I have, for the most part, deliberately avoided recommending particular makes and models of airgun for a specific purpose, as the market is constantly changing, and new developments may supersede even

tried and tested favourites in quite a short time, rendering any information that I may offer out of date very quickly. For this reason, I recommend that the newcomer makes an effort to study the equipment
which others are using, and to listen to their views, especially the views
of those who are clearly successful at their sport. Do not simply buy the
gun everyone else is using at a particular club. It may not necessarily be
the best gun for you, so be prepared to ask questions in a bid to find out
why one particular gun is so popular.

Points to Note in Achieving Accuracy

There are, in fact, relatively few top flight target air rifles which have
the features necessary for consistent pinpoint accuracy, i.e. placing successive shots through the same hole at 6 yards. Such a rifle needs to be
recoilless, superbly balanced, and matched carefully to the individual
who is to use it. For this reason you will find that competitions are
dominated by just a few specialist target weapons. Before laying out
your hard-earned money to buy one, be absolutely sure that you settle
for a gun which suits you in all respects, and is naturally capable of the
sort of accuracy which I have described.

When plinking, pinpoint accuracy is rather less important than in
competitive target shooting, and faults which develop in shooting technique can be overlooked to a degree. This is not the case in competitive
target shooting, however. Successful marksmen look for every possibility of improving their shooting to give them an edge to their performance, and perhaps clinch a match for them. Plinking can actually be
harmful rather than beneficial to good target shooting if bad habits are
allowed to continue unchecked. It is obviously necessary to recognise a
fault for what it is, before it can be corrected.

Stance is important. If the body is unbalanced or uncomfortable it will
not be possible to achieve the best scores consistently. If the stance is
wrong it becomes all too easy to hold the gun at various angles in
relation to the target without being aware of it. Stance can be studied in
detailed books on target shooting, but like many other aspects of airgun
shooting, a good stance owes much to common sense. If the feet are
placed far enough apart to ensure stability, and if the body is placed in
such a way that it is comfortable and so that the gun comes up on aim
smoothly and without wavering, then the main purpose of a good
stance will have been achieved.

Fitness One point which is not always fully understood, even by experienced shooters sometimes, is that it is necessary to be physically fit
in order to shoot well at competitive target shooting. Your blood needs
to be well supplied with oxygen to keep you alert and prevent dis-
turbances in the rhythm of your breathing, which will need to be moni-
tored carefully as you shoot. You should be fit enough to hold up the

rifle without swaying or wavering unduly. Although well balanced, a target air rifle is likely to weigh in excess of 10 pounds. This is a considerable weight when you bear in mind that you will be holding it in the aiming position to take a shot on numerous occasions during the course of a competition. Holding the gun on aim for too long, or even doing too much shooting at one time, can seriously affect accuracy, and will also show up any deficiencies in the shooter's personal fitness. With a target air rifle weighing in at around 10 pounds or so, any weaknesses in wrist, arm, shoulder, or other upper body muscles will quickly make themselves known.

Breathing Perhaps a good argument, if any were needed, in favour of competitive target shooting could be that it helps to keep you fit. A big beer belly and a persistent smoker's cough are not likely to boost you to the higher echelons of the competitive airgun marksmen.

Good breathing rhythm is important. Many beginners make the mistake of consciously holding their breath too long before they fire. This upsets the body's natural rhythm, altering heartbeat, causing deeper breaths to be taken to compensate, and depleting the body of oxygen temporarily. The shots should be taken during the natural break between breathing out and breathing in, and this break can be extended a little with practice. Exhaling should be gentle and measured as the gun is brought up to the aiming point, and the shot can then be taken when the lungs are empty.

The faults of snatching and flinching have already been described in chapter 4, and are common faults which need eliminating early on. Snatching is not always easy to correct, especially if the shooter is trying to avoid holding the gun on target for too long and is taking the shot before he is really ready.

Sighting When sighting pistols, the top of the foresight should be level with the top of the rearsight notch, and should be central in the rearsight. The sights should be horizontal and not placed at a slight angle; a good stance will help to achieve this. To be sure that the sights are aligned and set up as they should be, the aiming eye should be focused upon the sights rather than upon the target. As a result, the target itself will appear a little indistinct, but do not worry, that is perfectly correct; the sights are the important thing upon which to concentrate.

Hold A comfortable and steady hold of the rifle or pistol is also important and needs to be right so that movement is minimised and the sights readily aligned. It is possible to learn some aspects of hold by studying specialist shooting books but, as a general guide, if the gun feels comfortable and comes on aim quickly with the minimum of adjustment and, provided none of the faults mentioned exhibit themselves, it can usually be assumed that all is well. Avoid falling into the trap of becoming so familiar with a particular gun that you overlook any shortcomings. Be critical in self analysis and of your equipment. Take nothing for granted and you stand a good chance of turning in scores comparable with the best.

Choice of pellets When a target shooter reaches the stage of ironing out all the little imperfections in his equipment and in his own method of using it, he may possibly begin to be over concerned about the pellets he is using. The flat-headed 'wadcutter' type of pellet is generally used in indoor competitive target work as it gives a clean, non-ragged hole in the target card, making accurate scoring easier. Although a little less aerodynamically efficient than, say, pointed pellets, the wadcutters offer excellent accuracy at the ranges involved. At short range, velocity variations are rather academic, provided they occur only when the type of pellet used is changed, and not from shot to shot.

There is little point in spending a substantial amount of money on a top recoilless target air rifle, then using just any old pellets which happen to be on hand. The pellets you choose to use must be proven to be effective in your gun, and that, as far as target work is concerned, means that they must be very accurate. Should you be hunting, obviously you would look for pellets which are able to offer an acceptable muzzle energy when used in your gun, but for target work at the relatively short ranges involved, accuracy is all.

It is impossible to recommend any particular make or model of pellet, since the requirements of each gun, sometimes even of the same model, are different. The bores of German air rifles, for instance, while nominally the same as their British counterparts are actually fractionally different, so a broad guide is to use German pellets in German airguns, and British pellets in British airguns. This is something of an over-simplification, of course, and there are plenty of exceptions, but be sure of what they are before adopting a particular pellet.

The major problem with lead pellets is that, being of soft metal, they deform very easily, and it always surprises me that pellets supplied in tins, as most are now, are not more damaged than they usually turn out to be, especially when you consider how tightly packed they are. The possibility of using a deformed pellet, which obviously is going to be less accurate than a perfectly formed pellet, can be reduced in a number of ways.

Some manufacturers supply their pellets in dispensers which hold each individual pellet separately from its neighbours. This ensures that any deformity can only occur after the pellet has been removed from the dispenser; so a basic cause of the occasional flier is eliminated at the outset. Pellets packed in this way are more expensive than mass-packed ammunition, but you may feel the additional cost is worthwhile. It is no good using one make of pellet for practice though, then changing to another for the big competition. Stick to one type of pellet for all your practising and competitive shooting.

Careful hand selection of pellets, eliminating those with imperfections, is another way of improving the odds in your favour. A magnifying lens will help you to study the pellets in some detail, but very careful handling is essential in order to avoid damaging any previously undamaged pellets. The skirts of diabolo pellets are particularly prone to damage, and while a certain amount of edge distortion to a pellet may be removed by the pressure of air and the passage of the pellet through the barrel, it is better to avoid risking inaccuracy by eliminating these pellets at the outset, especially if an important competition is involved. *Weight*. Some matchmen even go so far as to weigh each pellet to separate out those that fall outside a given range of weights. Obviously, the variations under consideration are extremely small, and normal weighing equipment is not sensitive enough to do the job. If you have access to a chemical balance you may feel the effort involved in weight selecting your pellets to be worthwhile.

Should you be reasonably adept, it is possible to make a small balance device which will help to select pellets that comply with the requirements. All that is needed is a simple 'see-saw' type balance, made of suitably light materials and critically balanced. Some small items (such as grains of sugar or salt, or tiny staples from a stapling machine) are needed which will counter balance the pellet, and which can be added or taken away until the pellet is balanced, having tested a suitably sized sample for accuracy. All pellets can be tested to ensure that they balance the scales. Those that do not can be rejected as being outside acceptable limits.

The actual weight of the pellets which you test in this way is not critical, since, being of a particular calibre (.177 for target work) and of the same make, the variation is going to be extremely small indeed, especially with the top makes of pellet which you are likely to be using. What is really important is that all the pellets are the same, regardless of whether 'the same' means relatively heavy or relatively light.

Having selected a batch of pellets for uniformity, they need to be carefully protected until they are ready for use. The few manufacturers who supply individually packed pellets have solved the problem for you, but pellets from tins need to be individually packed. There are a number of suitable materials which can be used for this purpose: foam rubber and expanded polystyrene come readily to mind. The material preferred by flower arrangers will also protect pellets. Known as 'Oasis', this material is a type of foam which can easily be cut out or bored to make holes to take the pellets. Unfortunately, it does tend to be a little messy.

Sizing. Some shooters like to use a sizer on the pellets before loading them into the breech, and these devices help to ensure diametric consistency within a given batch of pellets. What they do is to even out any irregularities in the pellet surfaces which contact the barrel of the gun, and also ensure that each pellet is identical in diameter and thus conforms to the barrel of the gun when it is fired.

To some extent an airgun acts as its own pellet sizer. When an airgun is fired, a blast of air under considerable pressure hits the rear of the pellet which is seated in the breech. When a soft, hollow lead pellet is used, the air pressure behind it expands the skirt to some extent on firing, and so enables the pellet skirt to grip the rifling effectively, helping the pellet to conform to the barrel of the gun and eliminating leakage of air past the pellet, which would reduce the available power.

However, deformities in a pellet, particularly minor damage to the front driving band of the pellet, are unlikely to be much affected by the air pressure as the gun is fired, and as a result, any pellet with this type of damage, albeit slight, can prove to be a flier. A well made sizer can eliminate the fairly minor damage which may not be visible to the unaided eye. Hopefully you will have already weeded out any badly damaged pellets.

Seating device. Some shooters like to use a pellet seating device. Some airguns have a tapered breech, so that a pellet which is being loaded simply enters and seats itself in the correct place. With other airguns, a pellet can be placed in the breech, yet without a firm push part of the skirt of the pellet may project over the face of the breech. When this situation arises in a break-barrel air rifle or pistol, the pellet skirt can be pinched and distorted as the gun is closed, and this is obviously disastrous for accuracy. Sometimes these pellets can fall out completely without being seen, resulting in a 'dry' shot, which can damage some airguns, often irreparably, depending upon design.

Any small stick, or a thin pen or pencil, *may* be used to seat a pellet, but care must be used to prevent the slightest damage to the pellet in the process. The use of a device specially designed for the purpose will make sure that the pellet is inserted the same distance into the barrel each time, as this will ensure consistency.

I do not wish to give the impression that your shooting will not be successful unless you are heavily loaded with gadgets. That is certainly not the case; many successful airgunners use little more than their favourite airgun and a tin of pellets. It is as well to be aware of what accessories are available so that you can make up your own mind about their relative merits and demerits.

As discussed previously, the quality of your shooting will depend upon a number of contributory factors, including practice, preparation, personal skill, personal fitness, and quality of equipment.

This may seem a most formidable and an exceedingly complex challenge, but if the sport really does begin to feel like that to you then just take a metaphorical step back and look at it again – remember it is a very enjoyable sport.

CHAPTER SEVEN

THE
FIELD TARGET SHOOT

For many years, the only properly organised competitive airgun shooting to be found on any scale in Great Britain was in the indoor clubs and the pub bell target shoots. Anyone wanting to shoot in a match organised by an established airgun club was required to use only .177 calibre weapons, and to shoot at a fixed range of 6 yards or 10 metres, firing at card targets, unless shooting in the slightly less formal atmosphere of a bell target shoot.

Many airgun enthusiasts enjoyed the challenge of pitting their skill against others of similar ability, but found competitive target shooting a little restricting and lacking in variety. They tended, therefore, to compete with each other in small groups, often in the open air. They fired at the sort of targets which plinkers use every day – old cans, plasticine, toy soldiers and, of course, card targets like the match enthusiasts. They fired from a variety of different ranges, even trying long range shots to add interest to their sport and develop their skill.

There were those who felt that much outdoor shooting lacked the discipline imposed in formal target shooting. Yet many of these outdoor shooters believed that competitive airgun shooting could be very popular, if it were properly organised and if sensible safety rules were established to protect the public and those competing. They were proved right. Towards the end of the 1970s several field target competitions were set up under the sponsorship of one of the monthly airgun magazines, and under the watchful eye of several shooting organisations. With a shaky but enthusiastic start, organised competitive field target shooting had arrived. Of course, many clubs had already been field target shooting for some time, but now this branch of the sport really began to gain popularity on a national basis.

Field Target Events

The major field target shooting events, which are generally held on a regular basis, are advertised in the airgun magazines and in local gun shops, and usually a telephone number is given for event enquiries. If you feel the need to write to the organisers, or if the shoot requires advance entries to be made by post, please help the organisers by en-

Field target shoot – mixing with other enthusiasts with different types of gun.

closing a stamped addressed envelope. Entry fees are, on the whole, very reasonable, but if an organiser needs to reply to hundreds of applications, each requiring a stamp, then costs will escalate and this will obviously eventually need to be reflected in the entry fees to these events.

As with anything new, many first timers at a field target shoot are a little nervous. If they are competing, the quality of their performance may be diminished by anxiety, and by being unsure of what to expect. It can be unnerving competing against a large number of people, especially if the individual has previously shot alone.

I have always been a believer in 'testing the water' before plunging in to anything new, so my advice to a newcomer would be to visit a field target event without taking a gun, and simply wander around, see what individual ranges are available, how registration is carried out, and what sort of targets you will be required to shoot at. Take a camera with you and act as an interested observer. Talk to the competitors and find out what they think are the likely problems for that particular day.

Perhaps there is a strong cross-wind, or maybe the course has been set up so that the competitors have the sun in their eyes for much of the day. Maybe the firing point is very muddy, preventing comfortable prone or seated shooting, or possibly an unexpectedly high turnout of competitors has led to long queues for certain events. This is, unfortunately, a common situation at field target shoots, and one which can allow nervous competitors to become rather uptight and consequently to shoot poorly when their turn does eventually come.

Preparation for the Competition

When you are confident enough to take part in competitive field target shooting, the preparation for the event should take place over several weeks prior to the competition. You should be fully familiar with the gun which you intend using, and all your practice (and there should be plenty of it) should be carried out using only that particular gun. Select one brand of pellet which you know to suit your gun, remembering that accuracy counts for more than muzzle energy in a field target competition, then stick to using only that type of pellet. Use of a different pellet may require a change in the zeroing of the gun, so change should be avoided in the weeks leading up to a competition.

Checking performance of gun/sighting Obviously, any faults in the gun or its sighting system should be rectified well in advance of the event for which you are preparing. Check that all screws are tight and that there is no obvious play in the action which should not be present. Any lubrication of the gun is best done several weeks before the shoot, as excess lubricant will cause an airgun to 'diesel', i.e. the lubricant will ignite under compression, in the same way as a diesel engine. If it is severe, dieselling causes erratic shots and can even permanently damage an airgun. The velocity of the pellet fired from an airgun which is dieselling badly will be in excess of the standard velocity, though it will not be consistent, and accuracy will suffer. Most airgun enthusiasts over-lubricate their guns anyway. Modern weapons require very little attention – literally a few drops of lubricant every couple of tins of pellets is all that is needed, unless the manufacturer's instructions say otherwise.

The gun should be carefully zeroed some weeks before the shoot (see chapter 4 for advice on zeroing), and if a telescopic sight is used – I would highly recommend that it is for a field target shoot – then it should be firmly mounted so that it cannot slide back in use.

Practice Practice, then, is the order of the day, or more appropriately weeks, since the more practice you have with your chosen weapon, the better your chances of making a good showing at the actual event. Remember, many of these field target competitions are won not by top names in airgun shooting but by unknown shooters.

Do not be intimidated by the presence of well-known and successful marksmen at the shoot. After all, the whole object of the exercise is really to have fun, and you are not likely to do so if you are tense and nervous. Try to relax, pretend that you are just plinking in the back garden at home, and do your best.

When practising for such an event, make a point of shooting at different distances from the target, learning instinctively how much holdover to allow on a long shot. Set up targets, at, say, five metre intervals, and include some very close ones. These can be among the most difficult to hit, until you realise that your sights are unreliable at close ranges. The barrel of the gun is, inevitably, a certain distance below the sights and, as a consequence, the pellet strikes lower than you might expect it to. You need to compensate for this factor, which varies from gun to gun, depending upon the sight mounts. Fire at least three shots at each target, so that the pattern is established, and the number of centimetres holdover, or perhaps holdunder, relevant for your particular airgun at a given range will become apparent.

The more powerful the gun, the less holdover is likely to be needed on distance shots, and this can be an advantage. The use of a .177 calibre air rifle can ensure a flatter trajectory, but a good .22 hunting air rifle should not need a lot of adjustment over the distances involved in a field target event, if the gun has previously been zeroed, for, say, 25 metres. One of the obvious attractions of field target shooting is that you are not, generally, restricted to any particular calibre in competitions. You are likely, however, to be required to have your air rifle tested on a chronoscope to ensure that the muzzle velocity is not above the legal limit. This test normally applies only to the main event at these shoots, and not to any side shoots.

It pays to arrive early at a field target competition to allow yourself time to become familiar with the layout of the ranges in use on that particular day. There is no set format, and the ranges tend to be organised to fit in with any natural features which may be present – a quarry or shrubbery, for instance. You will have time to gauge the effect of the weather on the shooting; it can be understandably difficult to concentrate with rain trickling relentlessly down your neck, and blustery conditions can play havoc with the scores too, as can unusually bright sunlight shining directly into your eyes.

Clothing and equipment Bearing in mind these last points, you will obviously need to come suitably dressed for the weather when competing in events such as this. Some form of hat with a peak is a must to shade the eyes and aid concentration. If the weather is likely to become wet, or is wet when you actually leave, a fully waterproof jacket will be needed. One that is merely showerproofed will soon let water through if it is exposed to continuous rain, even fairly light rain, for any length of time. The proofed cotton type of coat is to be recommended, although it can become extremely hot if the weather turns warm.

Suitable clothing should be worn underneath in case the coat needs to be taken off during the day. It is surprising how cold the hands can become on what may seem at first to be quite a mild day, so gloves may be useful. Personally I use thermal mitts, as these keep my hands warm, yet allow the use of fingers for loading the gun, handling pellets, and so on.

If you prefer to sit or lie prone when shooting, you may need to take a sheet of polythene or something similar with you, especially if conditions are likely to be muddy. You may find that waterproof overtrousers help you to be more comfortable when shooting in soggy conditions, bearing in mind that these shoots continue for most of the day, and even light rain will eventually find its way into your clothing if you are not suitably attired. You will find that field target shooters are a hardy bunch of people, and are unlikely to be deterred by rainy conditions. You can usually be sure that the event which you plan to attend will not be cancelled owing to bad weather, except, of course, in absolutely exceptional circumstances, in which case, a telephone call to the organisers will soon establish whether the shoot is to be abandoned.

You may find sunglasses a help in an outdoor shoot, but you may also find that they make it more difficult to see the detail on the targets. The painted metal type of target commonly in use soon becomes an even greyish colour all over, making it difficult to pick out the required point of aim. It is for this reason, too, that telescopic sights are more appropriate than open sights at field target shoots; they help the natural vision to pick out the detail on a target. Sunglasses, if used, should be of a type designed specially for shooters, without excessively dark lenses.

Ensure before you set off for the shoot that you have food with you for the day, and perhaps a hot drink, or soup, in a vacuum flask. If you are hungry, or otherwise uncomfortable, your shooting will not be up to top standard. Give careful thought before you leave to what you are likely to require on the day; the gun and a tin of pellets are by no means the only requirements. It is best to put together everything you need on the night before the shoot, so that you are not rushing around at the last minute, and perhaps becoming flustered because of something you are unable to locate or have forgotten to get.

Registration, rules, safety The first port of call on arrival at a field target competition must be the 'headquarters'. This is the registration office and is usually a tent or a caravan. Inside the office, the rules pertaining to the shoot will be prominently displayed, and these should be carefully read and understood before any shooting is carried out, regardless of how many other similar events you may have already attended. The rules vary only slightly from shoot to shoot, but some clubs often include a clause of their own; for example, one club may limit the number of attempts at any one event whereas another may allow any number of attempts at the same contest. It is best to read the small print.

Safety is always prominent in any rules at a field target shooting competition, and anyone who is not prepared to comply with the rules, or acts in a manner likely to endanger others, will be firmly asked to leave. This is important both from the safety viewpoint and from the public relations angle, as field target shoots are frequently held in country parks or other places where the public has general, and often unrestricted, access. Any bad behaviour, especially if it is seen to be accepted by the organisers, is likely to cause prejudice against airgun users.

If you make a point of arriving well before the start of the competition you will have plenty of time to acquaint yourself with all the relevant rules, and also have some time for a preliminary look around and perhaps a chat with some of the other competitors.

The Different Ranges

A field target competition generally consists of a main shoot, usually set out in marked sections, or lanes, and any number of different side shoots, each offering variations of target and differing skill levels. There may also be a novelty shoot of some sort. A marshall is responsible for each section of the shoot, and he will look after you and instruct you in the requirements of his particular shoot as you reach the head of the queue. You should obtain a ticket from the registration office before setting off for the ranges, and this ticket should be presented to the range marshall as you start.

Field target shoot – the range.

Let us assume that you are to shoot on the main course first. You will pay for your ticket at the office, then submit your rifle for chronoscope testing, which is often carried out in the same tent as is used for the office. Provided your rifle is safely within the legal limit of twelve foot pounds muzzle energy, you then walk out to the ranges to look for the zeroing range.

Zeroing range When an airgun is taken from one environment, a warm room for instance, into another, perhaps a cold windswept quarry where the shoot is being held, changes take place which can affect its performance – metal components contract or expand, altering working clearances; lubricants change in viscosity; condensation can form, etc. Consequently, shooters who have religiously zeroed their guns before setting out, and have checked that all is well, may find that accuracy is not what they expect once they reach the range. This is particularly noticeable when weather conditions are extreme, and some makes and models of airgun are more susceptible to these changes than others.

If a gun is not used for a while excess lubricant can build up, especially if it has been over-lubricated initially. The first two or three shots from a stored airgun are often unreliable, both in terms of accuracy and of power, and it is certainly necessary to fire one or two shots into the ground before starting to shoot in earnest.

To help counter these problems, a zeroing range is provided where competitors can check that their guns are performing effectively, and adjust them if they are not. This excercise allows the airgun to be warmed up and the firing clears the excess lubricant. The preliminary shots should be disregarded when using the zeroing range.

The zeroing targets themselves may be ordinary card targets or simple coloured discs on a white card. These are excellent as they stand out well even in poor light. Take care when setting them out that everyone has finished firing. The range marshall will let you know when it is safe to go down to the target area, and there may be some helpers who are prepared to set out zeroing targets for the competitors. Take your time when zeroing and be sure that everything is absolutely right before proceeding to the main range.

The main range The main range will have targets set out at various distances, from just a few metres to about 40 metres or more, and for convenience and ease of operation, as well as to save time, they are usually of the re-settable type. The most popular type of field shooting target, and the one that has come to be accepted as the standard for the sport, is the silhouette of an animal or bird, e.g. a rat, rabbit, crow, or other generally accepted airgun quarry. This type of target is made of painted steel and has a circular cut out fitted with a disc. When this disc is hit, the whole target falls over and lies flat. If the pellet just hits the body of the target without striking the circle, which is about 2 inches in diameter, the target will not fall and the shot will not count as a hit. The broad basis for this system is that the metal targets simulate animals you might normally hunt in the wild, and as a humane kill is essential, you obviously need to be capable of placing your shot very accurately. This type of field target enables you to judge your expertise very well. You can buy these targets yourself, too, if you have the space and would like to practise at home or on your own shoot. Once the circle has been hit and the target has fallen, signalling a hit, the device can be reset by the range marshall, usually by pulling on a string attached to the target, or by electronic means.

After a competitor has fired at all of the targets in the first lane of the main shoot, the marshall will mark the competitor's ticket, which doubles as a score card, to show the score achieved on that particular lane. The competitor then passes on to the next lane, where he is met by another range marshall, and repeats the process until he emerges at the other end with a completed score card and, hopefully, a good final score.

It may be necessary for you to shoot at a specified time on the main course, in which case you should present yourself to the lane marshall in good time to avoid delaying others. If you are late you may forfeit your chance to compete in the main event. In addition, you are more likely to be flustered, and possibly out of breath – hardly an appropriate state to be in when you are expected to shoot a few moments later. You may, of course, be one of those people who never becomes at all flustered. But for the rest of us, the advice must be to be prepared at all times. This applies both to the final moments before shooting and to the preparation for the shoot on the preceding evening.

When it comes to the actual shooting, take your time and direct your attention solely to the task in hand. This is often easier said than done, especially if you are unused to competing, but with a little practice, and allowing yourself time – reasonable time – to take each shot, it is possible to ignore much of what is taking place around you and to concentrate on your shooting. There are individuals who take far too long over their shots, holding up other competitors for an unreasonable amount of time. This is unfortunate, because not only does it upset other competitors, but it also encourages organisers to insist on time limits, and people often do not shoot as well if they know that there is a fixed restriction on their time. I should point out that I am only referring to extreme cases, so there is no need to be unduly concerned about the time you take. Remember, though, that if you try and hold the sights on aim for too long there is a tendency for the gun to waver, especially if you are using a heavy hunting rifle. If you find this happens after aiming for a while, lower the rifle for a second then try again. Do not snap off the shot in the hope that it may be a good one.

I have seen competitors miss a shot after a run of success and then lose their concentration. In this respect the sport is much like any other,

say tennis or golf, for example. Competitors blame themselves for missing what they consider a straightforward, perhaps even easy shot, and
because they dwell upon what might have been, they fail to concentrate
on successive shots properly. As a result, the final score is well down
whereas it might have been one or two points below top score. The
problem is understandable, but you should try to overcome this by
treating each shot as the main shot. In other words, every shot you take
should be treated as the only one you are going to shoot on that day.
Forget those that have preceded it and those that will come later; give
your full attention to the shot you are taking at any one particular time.
It can be disheartening to miss two or three shots in a row, especially if
your earlier performance has been exemplary, but everyone does it at
some time or another, so avoid letting it affect the rest of your day's
shooting.

Side shoots Apart from the main event, each field target competition
has a number of side shoots. These vary in the skill level needed to
compete successfully, and will often include some sort of novelty shoot.
The vermin range may be like a small version of the main range, with
knock-down rats and rabbits peeping out from behind bushes and boul-
ders. If the terrain is suitable, you may well be expected to climb into
some awkward positions to take a shot, just as you would if you were
hunting the real animals depicted by the targets. You may also be required to take the same target from more than one different position, to
really test your skill in a simulated hunting situation. The targets will be
set out at all the ranges at which you would be expected to shoot if you
were actually hunting, with possibly an extra one or two placed out

A collector's gun at one of the side shoots.

beyond the normal range to add an additional challenge. Scoring is usually similar to the main event, with a fixed number of targets being shot. Side shoots may or may not carry prizes; some are provided for entertainment only, and to help reduce the strain of numbers competing at one time in the main event.

Novelty shoots There may be a rare chance to fire a collector's airgun, such as the long lasting and still much used Lincoln Jeffries rifles, or perhaps early Webley rifles which were so well made that many are still in regular service to this day. Since it is not usually possible to try these old guns beforehand, success is literally a hit or miss affair, but it is always valuable and enlightening to be able to try as many different airguns as possible. Be careful when using these old timers though. For obvious reasons they are irreplaceable, so handle them with the respect they deserve, even if they do look worn and tatty.

Pistol range You may like to try your hand at the pistol range. One of these is often provided, and you may find yourself shooting at card targets, at clay pigeons (discs of clay which shatter satisfyingly when hit), or even at tin cans. You may use your own pistol for this event, but one is normally provided for those who have only brought rifles but would like to try their hand at pistol shooting. This range may just be for fun or it may be possible to score and win a prize. Not many airgun shooters are proficient with a pistol so, if you have any sort of aptitude for air pistol shooting, you might find this well worth a try. 'Scopes *may* be permitted here.

Hidden target shoot There is a course which has been used with success at some shoots, and that is the 'hidden target' shoot. In this competition, targets are concealed at various points in the course, and competitors, accompanied by a range marshall, are required to find as many of the hidden targets as possible and to shoot at them. The number of targets hidden will not be made known before the shoot, so to pick up the maximum number of points available the competitor must rely heavily upon his own powers of observation, something he would need to do for successful hunting. Naturally, a varied terrain with plenty of natural cover is more appropriate for this type of shoot, because it is difficult to conceal targets on a closely cropped, flat grass meadow. To make life a little harder still, there is usually a time limit placed upon the hidden target shoot.

Snap shooting range One of my own favourite field target ranges is the snap shooting. It may go by other names, but is basically the same as the army snap shoots, where the competitor fires at a target, often the silhouette of a soldier, which only appears for a few seconds. The target is electronically operated, and lies flat for a measured number of seconds while the airgun is being loaded and cocked. It then stands up for several seconds while the shot is taken, and then lies flat again for reloading for the next shot. The duration of the rest period and the shooting time available can be controlled by the operator. The competitor may be required to take five shots in succession to score, and this range is a good test of reflexes. It is easy to be caught out by the target popping up before loading is completed. This necessitates a very hurried shot before the target disappears again, and the rhythm of shooting is upset, with detrimental results to the score. Rhythm really is the key to success in snap shooting, with a smooth cocking and loading movement being followed up by a relatively unhurried shot which is let off a second or so before the target is due to drop back down. It may pay to count off the seconds as other competitors are shooting, so that you have a reasonable idea of when the target is going to come up or fall back down. This is quite challenging shooting, and it is all too easy to drop a pellet while fumbling with the mechanism. Logically, then, all pellets should be readily to hand, and the shooter should be comfortably settled before starting. There are only three types of airgun suited to this type of shooting: break barrel rifles, which can be cocked and loaded quickly; repeating types which feed the pellet in automatically as the weapon is cocked; and those which use a pre-charged cartridge (provided the cartridge can be fed into the gun quickly enough between shots).

A variation on target snap shooting of the type described may be seen occasionally. That is a combination of the hidden target and the snap target, where targets pop up in unexpected places and remain for a few seconds before disappearing again. These electronically controlled targets are naturally expensive, and smaller clubs are unlikely to be able to afford to use them.

Decoy pigeons Heavy pellets are preferred for these plastic pigeons.

The number and variety of available side shoots at a field target competition is limited only by the imagination of the organisers and by the restrictions of the site chosen for the event. Some clubs are more inventive than others, some obviously have less money to spend and other clubs may have difficulty in obtaining a suitable site.

There is evidence that field target shooting is growing in respectability as it grows in popularity. Enthusiasts should support these events to show the public that airgun users are participants in a legitimate sport, and in pursuing that sport are able and indeed anxious to be seen acting in a responsible manner at all times.

CHAPTER EIGHT
HUNTING

The motivation to hunt is not altogether clear cut. It may well be a combination of things: the farmer may hunt to control a particular vermin species, perhaps wood pigeons which are ravaging his crops. Another individual, bored with pre-packed supermarket food, may really relish the thought of a fresh rabbit for the table, knowing that his dinner will not have lain in a deep freeze for months on end before being prepared.

Undoubtedly, the motive which provokes most controversy is that of hunting for sport, that is to say, hunting for the enjoyment of pitting one's wits against those of a wild animal. Man is, by nature, a predator, dominating animals to a greater or lesser degree, and the urge to hunt probably goes back many years to when man had to hunt to survive.

Those embarking on a hunt should remember that anyone who goes into the countryside and wilfully shoots at anything and everything that moves is both irresponsible and destructive. Such action quite rightly invokes public concern, and can do great harm to the image of airgun shooting as a sport.

Conservationists care deeply about the countryside and the preservation of wildlife, though it is not always understood that hunters themselves must also be conservationists. Obviously, there is no merit in killing off all the rabbits in an area. A shoot, as hunting land is termed, must be well managed and farmed to achieve a proper balance. This is the essence of good husbandry, and the basis of sensible hunting.

Assuming you have been successful in finding a shoot, the next task is to acquaint yourself with the terrain. Do not even consider shooting until you have first walked around every inch of the land *without* a gun. Observe and commit to memory every aspect of the ground, noting where wild creatures have been, or are likely to be, and recording areas of cover which may come in useful later.

Fieldcraft

As you do this, you will become aware that fieldcraft is a primary element of a successful hunt. You are not likely to be very successful unless you learn the ways of your quarry: its habits, what it likes to eat, how it detects and signals danger, what signs it leaves of its passing, etc. Carry fieldcraft to the ultimate conclusion and you will develop a deep affinity with nature, with a feeling of actually being an integral part of the natural world, like the people who work in the country all the time.

You need to be very much aware of your surroundings: avoid stepping on dry, noisy twigs, stay downwind of the quarry so that your scent is carried away from, and not towards, the animal. You may not think that you smell particularly strongly, but it might surprise you to know that a great number of animals are capable of detecting your presence from well over 100 metres away, if the wind is blowing from your direction to them; a thought well worth reflecting upon when you are stalking.

Most of all, though, patience is called for when embarking upon a hunt; if you are the impatient type, then hunting is definitely not for you. To be successful may entail sitting or lying motionless for an hour or more in an awkward position. Merely strolling around the countryside in the hope of finding something to shoot at is not just irresponsible, but is almost certainly doomed to failure. Develop proper fieldcraft skills, avoid shooting at everything that moves, and you will find that you become so engrossed in your surroundings that you have no time to be bored.

Part of the attraction of hunting must certainly lie in the skills involved in competing with nature, in pitting one's wits against creatures which have had to develop the art of survival to a fine degree.

I do a fair amount of my hunting with a camera and, though I would not have believed it possible when I was younger, I gain as much enjoyment from 'shooting' with a 35mm camera as with something more lethal. Apart from the actual shot itself, be it from airgun or camera, the rest of the hunt is virtually identical: the study of the terrain in advance for evidence of the quarry which is being sought; the preparation for the hunt (including the selection of appropriate equipment and camouflaged clothing, to ensure that the hunter blends in with the countryside); the detailed search for the quarry itself; the stalk (which may involve an hour or more of messy, uncomfortable crawling through brambles, ditches, and across sharp stones, possibly in pouring rain); and, finally, the 'kill'.

When a hunt has been approached methodically, with much preparation and observation, the eventual point when the trigger of the gun is squeezed is almost an anti-climax, signalling as it does the end of a whole series of enjoyable events.

What to Hunt

The question of what to hunt should be of concern to anyone contemplating the pursuit of living creatures with any sort of weapon.

Generally speaking, a creature which is regarded as a threat to the well-being of man for any reason is regarded as vermin, and as such considered fair game for the hunter. It may qualify as vermin by virtue of its taste for farm crops, or perhaps by its habit of creating dangerous burrows into which unsuspecting farm animals may stumble and be injured. It may block chimneys by building nests in awkward places, or steal the eggs and young of protected species of birds. It may damage young trees, and thus gain unpopularity with forestry workers. It may be a carrier of disease, contaminating stored feedstocks or destroying valuable crops or equipment.

Yet the fact that an animal or bird has been known to do any of these things does not necessarily mean it is classed as vermin, or that it should be relentlessly pursued as such. National law on the subject is not always clear or correctly interpreted, and local byelaws may exist which are relevant: an animal or bird which is regarded as vermin in one part of the country may not necessarily be viewed in the same way elsewhere. Sometimes farmers or ill-informed gamekeepers break the law by shooting protected species, such as birds of prey in the belief that those birds are vermin. Certainly, it is easy to see that birds of prey in any numbers could pose a threat to a well-run pheasant shoot, and as such might qualify for the 'vermin' tag, as far as the gamekeeper is concerned. As an intending hunter, you must consider that it is the law, not individual opinion, which lays down specifically what you may or may not hunt, even if that law may be interpreted differently from region to region. There have been cases where creatures generally considered to be vermin have been shot by airgun users and the action has resulted in a charge being brought by the local police (often in response to a complaint from a member of the public), and a fine from the magistrates has been known to follow.

The status of some species of vermin may even change depending on the time of day! The humble rabbit becomes, for the purposes of the law, 'game' under certain circumstances – after nightfall, for instance – and an offence may be committed when these animals are hunted after dusk, unless certain conditions are observed.

It will be clear, therefore, that a careful investigation of how the law is interpreted and operated in your own particular area is essential before embarking upon a hunting expedition. Bear in mind, too, that most wild birds are protected by law, and apart from a fine, anyone killing or injuring a protected species can expect to have his gun confiscated.

Where to Hunt

If your neighbour objects to you hunting, even on your own land, there is a provision in law for you to be brought to account if it can be shown that a nuisance or danger to the public has been caused. Always ex-cercise great care when shooting, and make enquiries with your local police force before setting off on a hunt. Make sure that you obtain the name of whichever officer advises you, in case of future reference.

Over the years, as a result of their destructive antics with airguns, some irresponsible individuals have succeeded in attracting the adverse attention of the press. The mention of airguns and hunting in the same sentence will usually result in instant criticism. Yet the right airgun, used at a sensible range by a marksman who has taken the trouble to ensure that his shooting is of a high standard before embarking upon a hunt, can be more humane than a shotgun, which, with its tiny pellets, can often fail to achieve a quick, clean kill, unless range and judgement of the shot are exactly right. The shotgun has attained a lofty position of respectability, while the airgun has achieved relatively little general acceptability within the hunting field, though it is widely respected as a target weapon. The reason for this is, I believe, guilt by association, with the public at large tending to link the airgun with the vandals who sometimes use them. This is, perhaps, somewhat unfair logic, since shotguns do not generally attract the blame when they are used in armed robbery.

It is not universally known, but there is little, if any, variation in effective range between a twelve bore shotgun and an air rifle with a muzzle energy near the legal limit. This fact has a little more to do with accuracy than velocity, though, since with a shotgun the 'holes' be-tween the shots become larger as the shot travels further from the barrel. It means that at extreme ranges, unless the shot misses the target completely, it is likely that only a single small shot may strike home, having perhaps insufficient engergy for a clean kill by itself.

A good quality, well-maintained, high powered air rifle may be justi-fiably regarded as a viable alternative to a shotgun, then, for vermin control purposes. If in doubt as to whether your own airgun is up to standard for vermin control, seek advice from your local gun shop, which may have facilities for your gun to be velocity tested on the premises – a facility which is becoming increasingly common.

It is important for anyone intending to go hunting to ensure that the standard of their shooting is sufficiently high to guarantee that the pellets reach the intended target. A fast and humane despatch should be the goal of every conscientious hunter, and this can only be achieved if the hunter practises constantly.

Practice should involve shooting at a variety of different targets of varying shape and size, and at different ranges and angles of fire. If possible, take your targets out to the shoot and set them up in areas where you might expect to find the vermin you intend to hunt. You can then shoot from the sort of angles and distances that you might expect to encounter when actually engaged in the hunt.

It will be of help to you to attend some field target shoots, too (see chapter 7). These offer the sort of varied open air target shooting which comes nearest to simulating conditions you may encounter in the hunt. You will find that if you do not practise for a week or so, your shooting may not be as good as you had expected. Constant practice is essential if you intend to hunt humanely.

How to Hunt

Having established what and where to hunt, it is next necessary to give thought to how. We have already seen that careful observation and preparation are needed when about to hunt, and that good field craft is a prerequisite for the successful hunter. In addition to general field craft, it will be essential to learn as much as possible about the habits of the individual vermin species being hunted. Where do they feed? What routes do they take to reach those feeding places? Are they exceptionally shy, or are they fairly used to people passing?

If you are hoping that your hunting will help the farmer who works the land over which you will be shooting, you have an additional avenue of approach. Any farmer who is having trouble with vermin, whether they are ravaging his crops or devastating his stored grain, will be sure to know where to look to find those vermin, and what their habits are. After all, he works the land every day and knows every inch of it, so a fact-finding conversation with the farmer before you start could be worth days of personal observation of the shoot. Do not be afraid to accept advice, because even if you spend all your life hunting, you will never learn all there is to know about the subject.

Hides and camouflage If it is your intention to shoot over one particular patch of land on a regular basis, it may be worth your while erecting a hide. This has a number of advantages. Provided the owner of the land has no objections to the erection of such a structure, a hide can provide the hunter with a relatively comfortable resting place while awaiting the arrival of the vermin, and can even be equipped with a waterproof roof if desired.

By virtue of its name, the function of a hide is to provide concealment for the hunter. However, it need not necessarily be camouflaged, because wildlife quickly becomes used to new structures, such as small sheds or stables, and tends either to ignore them completely after a few days or else use them as perching places.

The simplest form of hide is made by using the natural cover offered by existing bushes or thicket, and perhaps adding a few leafy branches to complete it. A bale of hay or straw makes a good seat, and could, if you wish, be used to construct a complete hide – especially useful in an area where there is little natural cover. A piece of old corrugated iron, perhaps covered with leafy branches would make a good roof.

There is really no limit to the variety of materials or different designs which may be used to construct a hide, although I feel that it is a challenge to be able to create one out of natural foliage wherever possible. That has the additional advantage of being less noticeable than a structure fabricated from man-made materials.

Remember to site your hide with regard to where you expect to find the quarry you seek, so obviously the preliminary reconnaissance is doubly essential here, especially if the hide is to be permanent. Ensure, too, that you have allowed yourself a wide field of fire from all angles without sacrificing concealment.

Try to view the scene as visualised by your quarry, and it will do much to help you be a more effective hunter. For instance, a wood pigeon homing in on a farmer's crop of brassicas would expect to see a quiet countryside scene with no visible humans close by, and nothing to deter it from its planned feast as it approaches.

Imagine, then, as it flies in for its meal over what it takes to be a stack of hay bales, it suddenly spots a pale blob moving about among the bales. Sensing that something is out of place with the scene, it quickly veers off and flies away in alarm.

The blob was the poorly concealed face of the hunter, and if you do not believe that a wood pigeon is capable of spotting a man's face from a long way away, then I suggest you put it to the test some time and prove to yourself just how uncannily observant these birds are. Much the same applies to other vermin, whose lives depend on their ability to detect and avoid trouble every day of their lives.

So the lesson is 'do not underestimate your quarry'. Camouflage clothing can obviously be of help when hunting – a bright shirt and fashionable trousers may look very fetching at the disco or as you stroll along the seafront, but the only wildlife which is likely to come anywhere near you if you wear the same gear on a hunting trip will be mosquitoes and wasps. Sober, even drab clothing blends in better with the surroundings in the countryside.

There is no need to spend a lot of money on camouflage equipment, unless of course you want to do so and have the cash to spare. An old shirt or jumper of a dull brown or green shade will help to ensure that you blend in with, rather than stand out from, the countryside. Match this with dark trousers and a hat of a similar shade, with maybe a peak to cover your eyes against the sun and shield your face from above. Add a pair of stout walking boots and you are in business.

It takes some nerve, but if you do not mind spreading stage make up or even mud over your face and the backs of your hands, and ignoring the fascinated or nervous stares of passers-by, the improvement in your hunting success rate may prove the exercise to be worthwhile. Of course, if your skin is already of a suitably dark hue then you have a built-in advantage.

Avoid taking out a white handkerchief when hunting – at least when you are in full view, as it will frighten away everything for miles around. Smokers will probably find it to their advantage to become non-smokers during a hunt because the smell of tobacco is very lingering and may well give away your position needlessly. Even with my relatively poor sense of smell, I can detect a smoker from hundreds of metres away when I am out shooting, so for any creature with a better sense of smell than humans, and that includes just about every vermin species apart from birds, the smell must be overpowering. That is not to say that smokers are necessarily unsuccessful hunters – if farmworkers regularly smoke in the area, the animals may have become used to the smell and it will not cause any alarm.

Calibre The question of calibre has already been covered (see chapter 2), and after weighing up the advantages and disadvantages of the available calibres it then falls to the individual to make a decision upon which calibre to use. Obviously, this is a decision which must be made when an airgun is purchased. If hunting is your likely goal, you must buy a gun in the calibre you deem to be appropriate, and of the specification which will do the job efficiently and be comfortable for you to use all day without exhausting you, either by its weight or by its poor balance.

Pellets In hunting, much the same rules apply to pellets as they do to competitive target shooting, or to any other kind of shooting for that matter. Find out what types of pellet suit your own particular gun and stick to them. By all means allow yourself to be wooed by the enticing claims of the advertisers for the latest line in hunting pellets – that is part of the enjoyment of the sport – but do all your testing and evaluating in the garden and on the practice range before venturing out on a hunt. You owe it to whatever you are hunting to shoot to the highest possible standard, and pellets are very much a part of that search for perfection.

Should you take a companion with you when you hunt? There are advantages and disadvantages in doing so, and it is worth looking at these before going ahead and inviting someone along with you to share your day's hunting.

When I lived in Wales I had perhaps a wider choice of places to hunt than is available in southern England where I now live. In some areas where I had permission to shoot, it was possible to walk all day through beautiful mountainous scenery and not see anyone else. In the event of an accident, a companion would have perhaps been a life saver, as it could take days to find an injured person in some of the remote areas in which I hunted. For the same reason, it is always a good idea to let someone know roughly where you are going when you embark upon a hunt.

Many people find it difficult to hunt without an accompanying friend, although personally I enjoy being alone, content to enjoy quietly the countryside around me.

A dog can be a good companion, but must be carefully trained not to race about uncontrollably, and to keep quiet when the hunt is in progress. Some breeds, such as labradors, make excellent retrievers, so they have a practical value in the field, but remember that they need a great deal of attention to ensure that they are trained to a good standard. Make sure you have both time and patience before acquiring a dog specifically to take hunting.

Returning to the subject of human companions, check to ensure that the owner of the land is prepared to allow you to take a companion with you. Make sure that whoever goes with you is a responsible individual who will respect the countryside code and not place in jeopardy your future chances of shooting over the land.

I have found that my most successful hunts are carried out when I am alone, partly because I prefer to hunt alone anyway. However, pleasant though it may be to have one or even more companions, unless you can work as a carefully co-ordinated team, you will find that the temptation to speak may be too much. If there are two of you, the chances of a giveaway cough or sneeze are doubled; two people make twice as much noise as one, and it does not require an expert in mathematics to realise that the chances of success are diminished in direct proportion to the number of individuals in the party.

Conservation

Should you be fortunate enough to have your own tract of land over which to shoot, or to have permission to shoot regularly over one particular piece of land, a great responsibility falls upon you. Hunters must be conservationists, land managers and wildlife experts all in one, conscious of which species of animals and birds inhabit the land over which they shoot, and concerned for the welfare of those species.

If that sounds a contradiction in terms let me assure you that it is not so. The indiscriminate destruction of wildlife lowers the moral esteem of anyone who engages in it, and that even applies to verminous species to some degree, since it is not for man to determine the balance of nature.

Occasionally, the balance does become upset, usually due to the activities of man. Pesticides can reduce the number of birds of prey, so allowing some of their natural prey to increase beyond normal numbers. Farmers' crops may be devastated and action may be essential. It is then that the skilled hunter with the appropriate airgun may show his worth and enjoy good sport at the same time.

Obviously, over-shooting an area will denude it of stock eventually, and even if the much maligned rat is the quarry, the simple fact is that once you have shot all the rats, assuming that were possible, which is unlikely, there will be none left to hunt.

On farmland, stock moves in naturally to replenish an area depleted by over-zealous hunting, but the process can take years. Be sensible and husband the resources carefully, giving thought to the future and having respect for wildlife.

Identifying Quarry

Hunters tend to become wildlife experts as a matter of course, since they come into contact with nature at first hand, and need to be able to identify clearly their quarry beyond doubt before squeezing the trigger.

To the inexperienced, the greedy, destructive wood pigeon can look much like a domestic racing pigeon or one of the rarer dove species when partly concealed among leafy branches. The hare, a game animal, can resemble the rabbit when only the long ears are showing above the grass. Acquire an illustrated field guide and study it carefully before hunting, to make sure that you are clear in your own mind exactly what you are hunting and, perhaps more importantly, what you could possibly mistake it for in the field under hunting conditions. Remember, the effect of the pellet is final; you cannot bring it back and start again, so if in doubt, do not shoot.

Accuracy

When you hunt, be sure that you can be certain of a head shot for a clean kill. Nothing less is acceptable. That means shooting at a sensible range; there really is no fixed 'effective range' for an air rifle, in spite of what some manufacturers might lead you to believe. Range depends upon many different factors, including type of gun and its condition, type of pellet used, effect of wind on the pellet, temperature, lubrication, accuracy of the gun, and so on.

Accuracy is far more important than power in any application, and no less so in hunting, although sufficient power is naturally a consideration. The most powerful airgun in the world is useless unless it is accurate enough to hit the target at exactly the point you intend.

If you have a large collection of airguns and tend to use them all, the chances are that you will never become fully proficient with any of them, so pick the one that will do the job and which is not going to be too heavy.

Pellets Match just one type of proven pellet with the gun and stick to that combination, because different pellets vary in their behaviour and often need slight sighting adjustment to take account of this. Any such adjustment is better made on the target range, where the results can be clearly seen and evaluated, than during a hunt, where any error could lead to unnecessary suffering.

Sights Open sights are acceptable for hunting provided that your shooting is of a reasonable standard, but it is generally accepted that a good quality telescopic sight is better, since it facilitates greater accuracy over longer ranges and also permits shooting in lower light levels than would be possible using open sights.

A word of warning, though: a telescopic sight will not necessarily help you to be a better shot. The standard of your shooting will still only be as good as the amount of practice you put in, so do not fit a telescopic sight with the idea that you will suddenly automatically begin to shoot like a top, world-class champion marksman. If you do, you may end up disappointed. Still, a telescope can certainly enable your natural skill to be exploited to its best effect, and to that end they are well worth fitting.

It is a fact that young people often shoot to an exceptionally high standard, with or without a telescopic sight, perhaps because they have more time available to practise. If you keep practising, your skill with an airgun will continue to improve.

Do not allow a telescopic sight to encourage you to take shots at excessive range when hunting. The limitations which apply to your particular airgun regarding inherent accuracy and velocity still apply when a telescope is in use; the only real difference is in the shooter's perception of range.

When buying a telescopic sight to be used for hunting, which is, in fact, its primary function, aim for quality, and avoid the cheaper 4 x 15 and 4 x 20 types. These have an inadequate field of view for hunting, and will certainly make the whole process of sighting a considerable strain under field conditions. A good 4 x 32 or 4 x 40, or similar, from a well-known manufacturer will prove to be the best investment.

When putting aside money for a telescopic sight do remember that the mounts usually have to be bought separately. You should check that the mounts you buy will fit your particular airgun, especially if it is one of the lesser known makes or models.

There are many useful types of sight available (see chapter 10 on accessories), some suitable for hunting, others less so, and some which are totally unsuitable. Seek advice before buying any type of sight other than the conventional sort already mentioned. When you have actually bought a suitable sight remember to test it thoroughly on the target range before venturing out on a hunt.

Safety One of the greatest areas of concern regarding hunting is that of safety. Each year there are accidents resulting in injury or death through the disregard for basic safety rules when hunting, so I make no excuse for mentioning safety again. Although many of the accidents relate to the use, or misuse, of shotguns, the principles involved are exactly the same and should be applied when hunting with airguns, which can be just as lethal as shotguns if misused.

It is not enough to assume that because you are shooting on your own land, or on land over which you have exclusive permission to shoot, that nobody else will venture there. Children in particular have a habit of investigating potential new play areas with great enthusiasm and disregard for the possible consequences, and a hunter who is totally engrossed in stalking may not see them enter the field of fire. Avoid shooting through bushes or shrubbery at low levels unless you are sure there is nobody behind, beyond your field of view. Quite often the sight or sound of someone hunting will attract youngsters who want to see what is going on. It goes without saying that you should stop shooting under these circumstances, although there is unlikely to be anything for you to shoot at anyway, since everything for miles around will have headed for cover at the first sign of approaching children.

Stay well clear of public walkways when hunting (see also chapter 1), and avoid shooting across routes taken by the public, since this is not only illegal but is highly dangerous.

First Aid

Hopefully, by observing these simple rules you will avoid injuring any-one. You may expect when you hunt to collect a variety of scratches, cuts and bruises yourself, from lying in awkward places and from worming your way through undergrowth. To avoid any wounds becoming infected it is worth carrying a small tin containing basic first aid necessities: some plasters, antiseptic cream, cotton wool, a small bandage and so on.

Like many other pursuits, you gain from hunting what you put into it, and if your approach is very casual and you trust to that fickle commod-ity, luck, you may not be too successful. You must be prepared to crawl around in muddy ditches, lie patiently for an hour or more, and gener-ally get yourself dirty and crumpled to achieve success. In my ex-perience, luck plays a very small part indeed, and those who work the hardest at what they do invariably make their own success.

CHAPTER NINE
MECHANICS OF THE MATTER

One of the pleasures of airgun shooting as a pastime lies not just in the shooting itself but in the preparation for the shooting. The same is, of course, true for many other hobbies and pursuits: fishing, sailing, metal detecting, and so on.

A word of warning: uninformed tinkering can lead to accidents involving serious injury. It should be clearly understood, *before* any attempt to dismantle an airgun is made, that spring powered air weapons have their mainspring under a certain amount of compression when the gun is not even cocked. These springs are strongly made, and hold a considerable amount of stored energy. The amount of this energy depends upon the type of gun. In some cases it is just enough to prevent an uncocked airgun from rattling, as it would with a loose spring. In others, the stored energy is very considerable, as the mainspring is under a fair amount of tension, the sudden release of which can be disastrous.

Airgun mainsprings can and do cause severe injury, and are quite capable of removing an eye, all in a fraction of an unguarded moment. When you are working on your gun adopt suitable precautions to protect yourself from similar injury.

Dismantling your Airgun

Many shooters are content to confine their attentions to careful polishing of the stock, occasional oiling of the action, and perhaps a little mild customising on the outside of the gun if they have the necessary skill. This sort of limited work can be every bit as satisfying in its own way as a total overhaul of an airgun, and one always seems to shoot better with a well prepared gun.

Yet it must be accepted that many of us regard airguns as exciting parcels, which must be quickly opened to view the contents. We enjoy the challenge of carefully dismantling a factory assembled weapon with a view to transmitting the same loving care to the inside of the airgun that we lavish on the outside – the parts that are on view to the world.

Sometimes we are stimulated purely by curiosity and a genuine desire to know how the gun works. More often, it is likely that we hope to improve in some way upon the factory produced article; to make an airgun more powerful; to make it smoother and more pleasurable to use; to improve upon a poor trigger mechanism; or perhaps to eliminate some other feature which we regard as undesirable and to introduce features which we would prefer to see.

It is not the purpose of this book to delve deeply into tuning procedures and stripping-down processes relating to specific makes of airgun, or to attempt to analyse the research which has been carried out in recent years in the area of airgun mechanisms and their function and improvement. These aspects have been adequately covered in several other excellent publications. My aim is to give the newcomer an insight into what to expect and what to avoid when working on airgun mechanisms.

Uninformed tinkering is not only dangerous but can also be very expensive. Modern air weapons may seem quite rugged and sturdy, but they are precision instruments like fine clocks or electronic equipment, and should be treated as such.

Start by obtaining as much information as possible about the airgun you propose to work on. Many manufacturers supply a data sheet with their products, giving a blown-up diagram of the various components, together with a spare parts list. These can help you to understand something about the way the gun works, and give some guidance to any special problems which may be encountered. Makers rarely provide much more than this. They prefer to advise owners to take their guns to a qualified gunsmith for maintenance. In fact, many gunsmiths derive much of their work from the failed attempts of an owner to repair or service his own gun.

The monthly airgun magazines are a good source of detailed information on the maintenance of specific weapons, and sooner or later all the more popular airguns come under scrutiny. The writer who carries out the work on behalf of the magazine will report on any problems encountered in the work, so that others attempting to do the same job will be forewarned, and thus able to avoid any expensive or dangerous pitfalls. There are other books, too, as I have mentioned, which delve in some detail into the stripping down and reassembly of various air weapons.

Some Misconceptions

It is a popular misconception among beginners to airgunning that in a spring powered air rifle or pistol the replacement of the original mainspring with a more powerful spring will result in a big increase in power. I recall, as a youngster, sawing up assorted springs and experimenting with different combinations and lengths of spring in an effort to achieve greater power. I did sometimes manage to produce a fair increase in power, but just as often that improvement would be accompanied by a considerable loss of accuracy as the gun jumped about wildly on discharge. Sometimes there would even be a loss of power, as other components fought a losing battle against the characteristics of a mainspring which was never designed for that particular gun.

Experiments have been made in enlarging the tranfer port on several airguns. This is the small hole, or tunnel, through which the compressed air travels from the cylinder to the pellet in the breech. Again, it was found that the characteristics of each gun were different, and although in some cases there was a power increase, in others there was a power loss, as the optimum size of the transfer port was exceeded. Guns modified in this way could easily be rendered as little more than scrap, making these experiments very costly indeed. Avoid uninformed experimentation unless you have a lot of money to throw away.

Friction and Lubrication

Any mechanical device with moving parts, be it an engine, a bicycle, or an airgun, is subject to friction. In simple terms, this is a phenomenon which causes contacting surfaces to try to stick together, rather than slide easily one against the other. Friction generates heat and accelerates wear. Some things, like brakes and clutches in cars, actually depend upon friction to operate. Some trigger mechanisms in guns, also, depend on a certain amount of friction to ensure that they work safely.

When it comes to metal-to-metal contact, though, friction is generally an enemy rather than a friend, and basic tuning has much to do with reducing friction on the internal mating surfaces of an airgun. This can be achieved in a number of ways, as follows.

Friction can be defeated by separating the mating metal surfaces with a lubricant. Traditionally, the lubricant has always been a type of oil or grease, and this has the dual purpose of defeating friction and at the same time reducing wear on the moving parts. In recent years, solid lubricants and silicone-based lubricants have become more popular in the field of airgun maintenance. Moly lubricants, based on slippery molybdenum compounds, have been used in the automotive industry for years, and the success of their application in airguns led to their fairly wide use by the mid to late 1970s, along with other space-age lubricants such as PTFE, which had previously found domestic service as a non-stick coating for saucepans and frying pans.

The so-called solid lubricants are carried in a carrier fluid which may be designed to evaporate once the lubricant is in place, or the carrier may itself be a lubricant, either a mineral oil or a silicone-based lubricant which will help to retain lubrication qualities if the film of solid lubricant should break down. Modern lubricants are often very specialised, that is to say they have been developed to do one particular job, and may not be appropriate in another application. A lubricant which is ideal for a piston and cylinder assembly on an airgun may, therefore, be totally unsuited to a trigger mechanism. It could even cause damage if used in the wrong place. For this reason, and because few of us have specialised knowledge in the field of lubrication, it is important to follow manufacturers' guidance when using any lubricants.

Tuning

How well the moving parts of an airgun operate in conjunction with one another depends not just upon lubrication. The better quality airguns are manufactured to exacting tolerances, and can be expected to perform well. However, even on these guns there may be some room for improvement. Cheaper guns are likely to vary in quality from one gun to the next on the same model, and there is scope for considerable improvements to be made by tuning.

Piston and cylinder The fit of a piston in a cylinder is critical, since if it is too tight it will not move freely and will thus restrict the available power, whereas if it is too loose a fit, or inaccurately machined, air may leak past the piston seal, again reducing available power. Work in this area is intended to ensure that the piston has as slippery a fit in the cylinder as possible, without being too loose. Peering into an airgun cylinder will often reveal scoring and unevenness on the cylinder walls, and this can be removed with *very mild* abrasives, and finished off to a high polish using a lightly abrasive metal polish cream. Metal-to-metal contact points between the piston and the cylinder should also be highly polished, and any attempts to rush this sort of work by using coarse abrasives will be doomed to failure. More damage is likely to be caused than will be eliminated. If you are short on patience, do not even attempt to start this sort of tuning work.

Any work carried out on the internal parts of an airgun must be done amid scrupulous cleanliness. Large supplies of clean rag, preferably cut from an old sheet, are very useful, and if abrasives have been used, no matter how fine, every trace of these must be removed using a solvent cleaner, such as methylated spirit, before re-assembly of the various parts. Failure to do so will simply mean that the abrasives continue to do their work even after the gun has been reassembled. While this may well be seen as the lazy man's way to tune an airgun, once the working surfaces are all smoothed down and bedded in, the abrasive will continue to work, accelerating wear to an alarming degree and shortening the life of the gun.

Special Tools

Preparation is the key to any work on the mechanical parts of an airgun and, having read available information on the gun which you intend working on, the next stage is to ensure that you are fully equipped to do the job. Occasionally, special tools may be needed, such as a steel drift to tap out securing pins, but some tools may be easily made or adapted from existing ones. Drill bits of the appropriate diameter are useful for drifting out pins, but care should be taken as bits are brittle and snap easily.

A set of good quality screwdrivers, including Phillips and electrical types, will be a mainstay of your toolkit. Many airguns can, in fact, be stripped down using little more than a single screwdriver. It is important that your screwdrivers are of good quality, as you are less likely to damage stubborn screws than you would with cheap tools. You may find that an impact screwdriver set, which gives added leverage by a smart tap with a small hammer or mallet may be a worthwhile buy, as some screw fittings, notably on the German weapons, can be difficult to remove without damage.

A good workbench with a vice that has soft jaws is another essential, and it should be remembered that an airgun cylinder should be treated gently or it can easily be damaged by a too enthusiastic application of the vice. A cloth and wooden inserts should protect the gun when it is being held in the vice, because the steel is very easily marked, and blueing does not need excessive encouragement to come off.

Pliers, a set of Allen keys, especially the small sizes, and some spanners will cover most needs. A few fine files and an oilstone will not go amiss, either. A mole wrench can be very useful as an extra pair of hands on occasions. However, it should be remembered that this tool, although very useful at times, is the classic 'butcher's' tool, and can wreak havoc on the metalwork of your shiny airgun, so save it for emergencies.

Should you intend to make the stripping down of spring powered airguns a regular occurrence, I would advise you to make up a spring clamp, or have one made for you. As previously mentioned, airgun mainsprings are under a certain amount of tension as fitted, and this tension is released by removal of the cylinder end cap, or whatever

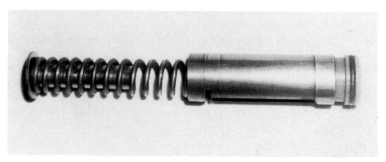

Piston and mainspring assembly from an air pistol.

similar device is fitted. A spring clamp pressurises the spring as the end cap is removed, then slowly releases the pressure, so that the mainspring can be safely removed. It is possible to make do without a spring clamp by placing the cylinder in the suitably protected jaws of a vice and then pushing down firmly on the end cap as it is being removed. A cloth placed over the cap will guard against its loss and give some protection if whatever you are using to remove the cap should slip. The big disadvantage of this method of mainspring removal is that – apart from being potentially dangerous – it is very easy to slip and for the spring to fly out. You have no way of knowing when the cap is going to come off, so you must maintain the pressure all the time. Unless you have worked on that type of gun before, you have no real way of gauging how much tension is on the spring, and on some air rifles it can be considerable.

The safe answer is to build a spring clamp. The requirements for this can be judged by examining the cylinder of the gun and taking appropriate measurements. Some sort of frame with a bolt which can be slowly unscrewed to release spring pressure can easily be devised, or perhaps adapted from an existing clamp. A good supply of solvent cleaner, lubricants and cleaning cloths will complete the workshop.

I would not advise work to be carried out on pump up guns unless you have successfully done so before. These guns are remarkably trouble free. Provided they are sensibly looked after, occasional lubrication, as directed by the manufacturer, is usually all that is needed. I have seen quite a few ruined by owners' inept workmanship, so if it is working well, my advice is to leave it alone.

Spring powered airguns, in their various guises, present few problems when dismantling. Where a safety catch is fitted, it is normally required to be on 'fire' to enable dismantling to be carried out. Stocks are removed by taking out the fixing screws which are usually quite visible. Watch out for the occasional hidden ones. These may be covered by a plastic insert, or let in from the bottom of the pistol grip, as with BSA guns.

Trigger Mechanisms

It is not generally necessary to dismantle trigger mechanisms when working on piston and cylinder assemblies, unless it is intended to make improvements to the trigger itself. This is a specialised job and should not be undertaken lightly. Some tuners polish the trigger sear to give a smoother trigger release, and the results can be quite a revelation to the shooter afterwards. However, a word of warning: some trigger mechanisms rely upon a certain amount of friction for their effective and safe operation. Elimination of this friction can be dangerous and cause the airgun to discharge spontaneously. The same can occur if adjustable triggers are over-adjusted to give an ultra light let off.

Fixing screws can sometimes be concealed as on this BSA Scorpion air pistol.

Piston detail showing a synthetic ring in place of the traditional leather washer.

Many trigger mechanisms are totally enclosed, such as the excellent trigger assembly fitted to Weihrauch rifles, and these are best left untouched unless you know exactly what you are doing. These are made to a very high standard, and there is likely to be little or nothing that an average unskilled owner can do to improve upon it. That is not to say that it cannot be improved upon – several specialists have taken up that challenge – but the job is not one for the layman.

Replacing Worn Parts

Air seal washers as fitted to break-barrel air rifles and pistols can be removed with a pin, preferably with a safety pin, and the groove into which the seal is fitted should be carefully scraped out using the same pin. Remains of the old seal, together with any specks of dirt which could prevent the new seal from seating properly, should be removed. The new seal should be fully pushed home and when correctly fitted should stand just proud of the breech face.

Any worn pins or bolts should be replaced, as should worn breech lock fittings, otherwise accuracy will suffer as a result of barrel movement. Damaged screws, bolts or safety catches should be replaced as a matter of course. The mainspring will also need to be replaced in time, and you may be surprised at how much longer the new spring is than the original one. Deterioration takes place over a long period and often goes unnoticed unless the owner makes regular use of the chronoscope. You may decide to invest in an individually produced spring from one of the specialist firms. Some of these are very good indeed and can greatly outlast the original spring. Should you adopt this course, you may find that the replacement spring in this case is actually shorter than the original. This is not a mistake, it is just that the characteristics of the new spring are different from the original, and it may be made from thicker steel wire, or from wire having a different profile, perhaps square sectioned.

When replacing a mainspring, I coat the whole spring in a moly based grease. This dampens any movement of the spring on dishcharge, makes the gun altogether smoother and really very pleasant to shoot, and eliminates the 'twang' which is the hallmark of many airguns. I use various appropriate moly lubricants when putting piston and cylinder assemblies together, and use a more conventional light oil on trigger mechanisms.

Every gunsmith has his own favourite concoction of lubricants, often mixed up to a jealously guarded formula. The important thing, as previously stressed, is not to overdo lubrication. This can cause as many problems as it cures: detonation, loss of power, fouling of the barrel, etc. Use lubricants sparingly and keep your work spotlessly clean at all times. Just a trace of grit can cause considerable damage if not quickly removed. It eventually becomes ground down to a fine grinding paste, which shortens the life of your gun. After reassembly, a light film of oil or rust inhibitor on all the metal surfaces will help them to remain rust free.

Incidentally, when applying moly lubricants to the cylinder walls of an airgun, the lubricant should be rubbed into the metal, rather than just smeared on. Moly based lubricants have some interesting properties, one of which is that they actually form a kind of bond with the metal, so in this respect they differ greatly from oils and greases.

There can surely be few situations as unsettling as dismantling an airgun completely, carrying out whatever work is necessary, preparing to reassemble the gun, and then finding that you are left with a heap of screws, bolts, and other components, with no clear idea as to how they should be reassembled. Sometimes after reassembling a gun completely a single solitary little spring or small screw may be left. The gun seems

A dismantled airgun.

to work all right, yet at the back of your mind you know that the manufacturer would hardly provide that component if it were not needed.

Problems of this kind can be avoided in a number of ways. Before starting work on any job which involves dismantling mechanical parts for the first time, have a pencil and paper handy to detail each step as it is taken. This can be done by listing each stage under a number. For instance, you may write: No. 1: remove three screws holding stock to action. No. 2: put the screws in box A.

This brings us to the second stage of avoiding chaos. Obtain an assortment of containers for holding screws, pins, springs, etc. Old pellet tins are very useful for the purpose, and if you buy some stick-on white labels from the stationers you will be able to number or letter the containers for instant identification. Be systematic at all stages of the operation and you will make life very much easier for yourself. Loose screws lying around on a work bench are easily knocked off and lost, too, and many of these are not easily replaced, having been specially made for their particular purpose. If you place them carefully in containers, the chance of their becoming lost is greatly reduced.

Fortunately, airguns contain relatively few individual parts, so unless you propose to be ambitious and dismantle a complex trigger mechanism, you should not meet with too many problems. Remember though, that even with few component parts, if you spread the work over more than a day it is very easy to forget what goes where. Sometimes you meet a component which can be put on in more than one way, though only one of those ways is actually correct. Should this be the case, you would be wise to mark the component to indicate which way round it should be fitted. Typewriter correction fluid is useful here, and it comes in a convenient little bottle with its own brush.

The amount of work which can be carried out by an owner on his own gun depends very much upon his individual ability and whether the type of gun lends itself to the relevant degree of home handiwork. Some jobs are best left to a well equipped workshop. It is possible to straighten a bent gun barrel in a home workshop, but this is not a job to be lightly undertaken since it is relatively easy to make the problem worse by putting an additional bend further down the barrel. Any work requiring machining, brazing, or welding is best carried out by someone who has the appropriate equipment and the necessary expertise.

It is relatively easy for an owner to make and fit his own leather washers and air seal washers. I buy old leather belts or handbags for a few pence in jumble sales, and the leather lasts for ages. I also use it to produce useful accessories, such as a holster for a pistol.

CHAPTER TEN

ACCESSORIES

Accessories fall broadly into two categories: the items which can actually add to the standard of your shooting, such as telescopic sights, pellet sizers and tuning kits; and items which make no difference at all to your shooting, but which are nevertheless satisfying to possess. The latter group includes pellet holders, plinking targets and polish for the stock of the gun.

Some might argue that even items which have no obvious direct bearing on the performance of the gun or that of the shooter may still improve his shooting by making him more comfortable, thereby improving his concentration. An example would be protective clothing. Someone who has confidence in his own equipment and its reliability will, naturally, perform better than the shooter who is forever having to tighten screws or make adjustments. It really comes down to deciding, firstly, what you would like, and then what you can afford.

Fortunately, as with most pastimes, once the essentials have been purchased, other useful items can be added to the collection in a piecemeal fashion over the years.

Protective Clothing

Arguably, one of the most important accessories, and that which commands a substantial share of the market, is protective clothing. Before buying special clothing, take stock of what your requirements really are, just as you did when choosing a gun. That way you will avoid wasting money on inessentials or unsuitable equipment. If, for instance, your interest is strictly plinking, and you never venture out in wet or very cold weather, there is no need to purchase special clothing: an old anorak will suffice. Perhaps all you need is a hat with a brim to shade your eyes from the sun, and maybe a pair of gloves to keep your hands warm on a chilly day. One of my own best buys was a pair of thermal mitts – open fingered to allow easy handling of fiddly pellets, yet still quite snug on a cold day.

If you intend hunting in all weathers it is worth considering thermal underwear. It can actually improve your shooting by allowing you to concentrate on what you are doing, instead of agonising over the bone-numbing cold seeping relentlessly though your thin clothing.

Camouflage-type outer clothing is fine for hunting, but make sure that it is also waterproof, not just showerproof, and that it has a degree of resistance to thorns and brambles. It should also have a thick lining for added warmth, and ideally this should be removable to avoid discomfort in warm weather. The waxed cotton 'keeper' type coats, with good deep pockets and effective waterproofing are an excellent buy, and are available in shades of green and brown which blend in well with the countryside.

Once you have a good jacket, and perhaps a hat with a peak to keep the sun out of your eyes and flaps to pull down over your ears, you have the main basic clothing. You may then decide whether to add waterproof overtrousers to complete the outfit.

Match shooters can buy a mitt to support the gun, clothing padded in various interesting places, barrel weights, a peaked cap to shade the eyes, ear muffs to eliminate distracting noises, and even special shooting spectacles to help the shooting eye to focus on the sights rather than the target itself.

Footwear is worthy of close consideration, especially for the hunter. During the summer I am always torn between wearing light sports shoes, like trainers, to facilitate quiet, light-footed stalking, and more substantial footwear, such as some form of boot. The type of terrain likely to be encountered will obviously have much to do with the final choice. If the ground is likely to be at all soft and marshy, then a strong pair of waterproof walking boots will prove a useful choice.

Wellingtons are not the best choice when out shooting, unless the terrain really is extremely soggy, because they are uncomfortable to walk in for any distance and give little support to the ankles. If you feel the need to wear wellingtons, invest in a pair of woollen sea-boot stockings to help cushion the boots and absorb perspiration. These extra long, thick socks should also be worn with other types of boot. Remember to allow for their thickness when selecting your boot size.

Tinted glasses are a popular accessory with match shooters, and worth a try if strong light tends to affect your eyes.

Telescopic Sights

Just about the first accessory bought by anyone with an air rifle is a telescopic sight. Perhaps I should clear up a few misconceptions regarding 'scopes before going on to consider what is available. A 'scope will not necessarily improve your shooting; if you shoot poorly with open sights then you will also shoot poorly with a telescopic sight. There is no magic property to a 'scope which will make anyone an instant expert, but used properly it can add a new dimension to your shooting.

Sighting can be a little slower with a 'scope, and the expense is prob-

Telescopic sight.

ably not justified for casual plinking sessions, particularly as some 'scopes will not focus down below 4 or 5 metres – the distance at which many back yard plinkers may do much of their shooting.

For hunting, however, a good telescopic sight can make the best of fading light, giving useful extra hunting time. Properly set up, it will give just enough magnification to allow clean head shots on rabbits and other vermin at a sensible range.

Telescopic sights range in price from single figures for a little 4 x 15 or 4 x 20 'scope (which is sometimes supplied with a gun as part of a package deal – usually in mail order catalogues) to treble figures for precision instruments with zoom facilities.

Most confusing to a beginner are the strange numbers identifying the various 'scopes. The first number indicates the magnification – 4 x is about right for airguns – while the second figure identifies the size of the objective lens. The larger this second number, the more light enters the instrument, and the greater the area which can be viewed through the sight.

Resist the temptation to go for high magnification, in the hope that you will be able to shoot individual feathers off wood pigeons at 100 metres. With an excessively high magnification, all that will happen will be that you will spend a very long time just trying to find the target through the 'scope. Even the benefits of a large objective lens will be cancelled out by too great a magnification. When you do eventually pick out the target, it will seem to be jumping around wildly, with every tiny movement you make translating itself into much bigger movements through the instrument.

Avoid the very cheap telescopic sights, and also the expensive, gimmicky 'scopes with lots of interesting, but often unnecessary features. A good make of 4 x 32 or 4 x 40 instrument will prove an effective choice for most eventualities.

Protection for Your Gun

Protect your expensive air rifle with a sturdy, waterproof gun cover. This will help to prevent scratches and scrapes while the weapon is being transported, or while it is in the cupboard at home. Small cases are available for pistols, although you may like to try making your own. Quality is very much related to price with gun covers. A good cover is not cheap, but can be expected to last the life of the gun, and even longer.

Velocity Testing

Those who become deeply involved in airguns as a sport will sooner or later want to be able to test the velocity of their gun, or guns. There are a number of reasons for velocity testing, apart from just being interested in knowing the performance of a particular gun out of curiosity. The performance of a spring air weapon falls off over a period of time. There are several reasons for this: the mainspring becoming tired, air seals beginning to leak, piston washers wearing and allowing air to pass on the compression stroke, and simply general wear. Often a new mainspring and a replacement air seal washer will be all that is needed to restore peak performance.

A gun's performance, like that of a car, can deteriorate so slowly over a long period of time that it is hardly noticeable and some means of measuring the power loss is useful. This is particularly important to the hunter, who relies on an adequate velocity to achieve clean kills.

The muzzle energy output of an airgun must be within the legal limit, and this is often tested at field target events, so an enthusiastic owner, who enjoys working on his own gun, must have the means of velocity testing, both to stay within the law and to avoid disqualification from such events.

Chronoscope/chronograph An airgun which is inconsistent from shot to shot as regards power is likely to be equally inconsistent as regards accuracy. Correct lubrication can eliminate the problem, but it is vital to know when the difficulty has been solved. To discover this a chronoscope, sometimes called a chronograph, is used.

The chronoscope is an electronic device with two sensors set at a fixed distance apart. When a pellet is fired between the sensors, the instrument measures the time the pellet takes between the two, and from this the velocity can be calculated – either manually, using a conversion factor supplied with the chronoscope or, in the case of a top quality instrument, in the chronoscope itself.

Since chronoscopes cost as much as a good air rifle, the outlay is not really justified unless you have a business dealing in airguns, or have a large personal collection of guns.

Ballistic pendulum/sledge A cheaper way of gaining an idea of the velocity of your gun is to use a ballistic pendulum, or a ballistic sledge. With the former, a pellet is fired into a metal cup on the end of a pendulum, which moves a needle on a gauge. The readout can then be used to calculate the velocity.

The ballistic sledge operates similarly, but more directly. Ballistic pendulums and ballistic sledges are accurate enough to give a fair guide, but cannot compare with a chronoscope for consistency. They are dependent upon careful use, and are subject to variations due to friction and temperature fluctuations.

Ballistic putty For those looking for a rough guide, ballistic putty is available. This is like plasticine in consistency. Pellets are fired into it, and comparisons made between penetration depths. It has a use as a comparative medium for tests between similar guns which are being tried out at about the same time. The results are subject to considerable variations in consistency, as the putty softens when handled. It does, however, make good plinking targets.

When carrying out velocity testing, be sure to adopt a procedure of firing a number of shots, eliminating any very high or very low readings, then taking an average of those left.

Targets

There are many different types of target available, ranging from conventional competition card targets, to cards depicting various types of vermin. There are purpose-built plinking ranges of steel construction, with re-settable targets and built in pellet traps. Electronic ranges are also available for those looking for something a little special.

Decoys and Camouflage

Hunters are a good market for the accessory manufacturers, and for those who take their hunting seriously, the range of goods available is considerable, since, to a degree, it also takes into account the large number of shotgun users.

Enthusiasts will not just shoot their quarry; they first hide from it in a hide constructed with Ministry of Defence surplus camouflage netting. The quarry is then encouraged into the general area with a specially made call, which guarantees to sound just like the real thing if used skilfully. You can call crows, ducks, and others, but not rabbits as yet, though I am sure the manufacturers are working on it!

If the quarry is wood pigeon or duck, it may be fooled into thinking that it is safe to feed by the sight of what it takes to be several of its fellows apparently enjoying a hearty meal. These are actually specially made decoys of plastic, wood, fibre glass, or even cardboard. A science has evolved around the question of how decoys should be set up, in which direction and in what attitude. The determined hunter will even put one up a tree if he is hunting pigeons in an effort to simulate the 'lookout', which feeding birds always rely upon to warn them of impending danger.

Having lured the hapless bird, the hunter will then take aim through his electronic red dot sight, or telescopic sight, squeeze the carefully adjusted trigger, and send a cleverly designed two piece hunting pellet on its way to despatch the bird.

If his quarry is a rabbit, the hunter will know that gutting, or paunching, is best done straight away, and for this he uses a carefully honed, multi-purpose survival knife, which is often nearly as expensive as the rifle. He then threads the rabbit onto a game carrier's loop.

It is easy to dismiss camouflaging as a gimmick, but if done properly, it can be staggeringly effective. I bought a camouflage suit at a game fair a few years ago, and used it on an evening rabbit hunt some time later. I was standing motionless next to a sycamore tree, waiting for a rabbit to show, when a buzzard wheeled in and flapped around within literally a foot or so of my head. This was quite an unnerving experience and I thought the bird may have been trying to intimidate me, but it flew to another tree just a few metres away and began preening itself. Clearly it had not seen me.

Tuning Kits

Maintenance should be restricted to occasional oiling of moving joints, and a few drops of moly lubricant introduced to the cylinder from underneath, or from the transfer port. This must be used very sparingly, or, as we have already mentioned, a phenomenon known as dieselling or detonation will occur. Excessive lubricant ignites with a louder than usual crack, and can seriously damage a gun if allowed to happen very often.

If you still prefer to work on your own gun with a view to improving its efficiency and smoothness, you can buy tuning kits which provide the necessary equipment and instructions to enable you to carry out the work yourself.

Silencers

Since the early 1980s, silencers have gained a degree of popularity, with several manufacturers now producing them, usually as a sideline to some other product. Silencers assist in reducing the blast as the pellet leaves the barrel, an effect which is more marked in some guns than others. They can obviously do nothing to reduce mechanical noise, which can be a fair proportion of the overall noise in a spring operated weapon. This mechanical noise can be reduced by use of one of the tuning kits already mentioned.

It stands to reason then that silencers are most effective on guns having a fairly noisy muzzle blast. The improvement on some pump up guns can be quite significant, since they have relatively little mechanical noise on discharge. The improvement is usually more noticeable to a bystander than to the actual shooter. Silencers can have a very small effect upon the accuracy of an airgun, and perhaps on the power, too. This is likely to be due to turbulence, or to the diffusion of the air propelling the pellet. The effect is minimal, however, and some makers claim to have eliminated the problem completely.

Pellets/Sizers

The number of types of pellet on the market is vast. Try them all, but then stick to just one or two types, or the consistency of your shooting may suffer. Lead pellets are easily damaged, and a pellet sizer will ensure the consistent size and shape of each pellet if you have the time to use such a device. Sizers appeal to target shooters, who are more inclined to inspect each pellet closely for the slightest imperfection.

Trigger Shoe

A tiny but useful accessory is a trigger shoe which, as the name implies, fits over the standard trigger to give a greater feeling of control. This in turn can improve accuracy. It is an excellent accessory, and is helpful if your gun does not have an adjustable trigger.

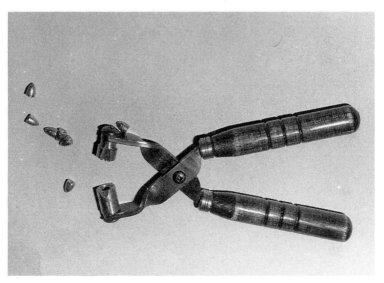

A simple pellet mould.

A selection of pellets.

Magazines/Books

The number of publications relating to airguns is fairly small at present, but the quality of those on the market is excellent, and they are well researched and informative. The monthly national magazines are a very good way of staying in touch with current trends and prices, and they are worth compiling into a binder for reference purposes.

The list of accessories is almost endless, and part of the enjoyment of airgun shooting is in browsing around the local gun shop.

CHAPTER ELEVEN
REFINISHING AND CUSTOMISING

Own an airgun and sooner or later you will probably want to work on it, to improve its appearance or performance. I do not propose to deal in detail with the dismantling of specific airgun mechanisms, but there are a few hints which would-be customisers may find useful.

Repairing and Refinishing the Stock

No matter how well looked after, any gun will eventually collect a share of dents and scratches, and these are probably best ignored until they begin to make the gun unsightly. Dents in wooden gun stocks can be removed quickly by applying a hot iron to a wet cloth placed over the damaged area. The steam encourages the wood to swell, drawing out the impression. In the case of a very large dent, the operation may need repeating a few times. After treatment, be sure to allow the wood to dry thoroughly before refinishing. If the dent is too big or stubborn to respond to this treatment, the only course is to fill it with plastic wood and then to use a darker varnish to hide the inevitable colour variation.

Before carrying out any work on the stock of a gun, you should be aware that the commonest stocks, made from beech wood, are usually given a colour varnish, or even stained, by the manufacturers. This will be apparent if the stock is scratched, since the colour shows through as a lighter shade. It will be obvious that simply touching in damaged areas with clear varnish is not likely to conceal blemishes fully. The answer is to remove the stock from the gun and sand it down completely.

It is usually obvious from a detailed inspection of the gun which screws need to be removed to detach the stock from the action. Watch out for screws fitted from under the pistol grip section; these may be concealed beneath a removable plastic plate. Once the stock is off the gun, all the varnish should be carefully removed by sanding with a medium grade glass-paper. Avoid using an extremely coarse grade in an effort to speed up the job as this can cause deep scoring, which in turn can be difficult and time-consuming to remove.

Be prepared to spend a long time, several evenings, if necessary, in preparing the stock for refinishing. After the main varnish has been removed, use successively finer grades of glass-paper to achieve a very smooth finish, rubbing out scratches as you go along. Ensure that your hands are clean and free from grease while doing this work, or you may find that the new varnish may not take properly. For the same reason, be sure that every last layer of the old varnish is removed, in case it is incompatible with the new. This may result in a wrinkling effect.

I suggest you use polyurethane for the new varnish, as it is very resistant to scratching and various solvents which may accidentally find their way on to the gun. This type of finish can be bought with an incorporated stain if you do not want to use a clear finish.

Varnishing Using a very clean, dust-free brush, put on a single, thin coat, and leave in a warm place overnight. When the varnish is completely dry, rub the stock with a very fine grade 'wet or dry' paper, used slightly wet, until the surface of the stock feels smooth. Although it will seem that you have undone all your work by removing the varnish, what you have actually done is to fill the grain of the wood, in preparation for the finishing coats. Five or six of these finishing coats will then be needed, rubbing down very lightly between each one to avoid a build-up of dust or unevenness on the surface. Keep each coat as thin as possible, or unsightly runs and streaks could appear. If you are a hunter and want to avoid the gun being too shiny, use an 'eggshell' or matt final coat. If using a gloss finish, the final coat should be deep, smooth, and free from blemishes. If there are specks of dust on the surface, wait for a few days for the varnish to harden fully, then burnish the surface, using an abrasive metal polish, working on a tiny area at a time. Finish off with a wax polish.

Inlaying An idea which you may like to try if your are re-varnishing the stock is to buy a piece of thin dowelling from the local do-it-yourself store; a piece about the thickness of a pencil will do. The stock of your gun can be drilled using a suitable sized bit to a depth of a few millimetres to take a section of dowelling. This should be stuck in using a resin woodworking adhesive, leaving a small amount of dowelling protruding. After an hour or two to allow the adhesive to dry, the protruding dowelling can be trimmed off flush with the surface, using a sharp wood chisel, and then sanded. If you stain the dowelling an appropriate contrasting colour before use, when the whole thing is varnished the inlaid dowelling will stand out as a feature of the stock. With a little imagination, sections of dowelling can be arranged into geometric patterns, or even your initials if you prefer. The whole job is cheap, and quite easy to do, but test on an old piece of wood first in case your drill is not quite the right size – it must be spot on.

This process involving dowelling is a technique known as inlaying and, if you have the confidence and the ability, you can expand the idea by making designs out of thin pieces of contrasting coloured wood. Trace round these on to the stock of the gun, and carefully cut out the exact shape using a very sharp craft knife. Scrape out the area to a depth of a millimetre or so, using a sharp chisel, and stick in the shaped piece of wood. Once the adhesive has dried, as with the dowelling, the proud surface of the wood can then be planed and sanded down to the level of the rest of the stock.

You may be able to buy small pieces of mother-of-pearl from larger music shops. This material is used extensively by musical instrument makers for inlaying, and can look very attractive when set in a dark wood background. Handle it carefully though, as it is extremely brittle and snaps easily.

Perhaps you do not feel confident enough to inlay your gun stock, but would still like it to look a bit different. The Royal Society for the Protection of Birds occasionally market rub-down transfers depicting different bird species, and these can look very striking on a gun stock. A coat of clear varnish will stop them washing away at the first hint of rain, and also lend protection against abrasion.

Why not paint motifs or animal silhouettes on to the stock? Many stationers and fancy goods shops stock stencils with a variety of interesting patterns which could be used for the purpose. Test whatever paint you intend to use on a small area first to ensure compatability with the existing finish. Degrease the stock carefully before painting, ensuring that there are no residues of wax polish left, then lightly sand the area to be painted to ensure a good key for the paint. As with all other jobs of this type, practise first on something other than your treasured gun stock, then, when your technique is satisfactory, apply your new skill to the stock itself.

Replacing pistol grips Pistol shooters often find that the standard butt grips supplied with the pistol are usually less than ideal, and would like to change them. Some of the more expensive air pistols have modified grips available as optional extras, but it is not too difficult to make your own if you wish, or if modified grips are not available. Many types of close-grained hardwood are suitable for the purpose, and a timber merchant should be able to find you a small offcut of walnut, mahogany, beech, maple or something equally suitable.

The usual deficiency with standard grips is that they are 'universal' – designed to suit almost everyone reasonably well, but almost nobody very well. Pack thin layers of well worked, warm plasticine around the original butt grips, then squeeze the grips firmly until the plasticine takes on the shape of your shooting hand and the pistol feels comfortable to you. The new grips can be carefully worked using chisels and perhaps sanding discs in an electric drill, shaping the grips gradually to conform to the plasticine pattern. If you are in your early teens you may need to do the job again in a year or two as you grow.

If you feel adventurous, you could try making butt grips from papier mâché. It needs a lot of patience, but this medium is actually extremely strong and malleable. A craft book from the local library will help you. I have just finished constructing a guitar case from this material, and the result is strong, light, and attractive. Instead of painting the finished case, I simply gave it a coat of clear varnish, leaving the strips of newspaper which formed the mâché as a decorative feature. It is a real attention grabber. Papier mâché, when dry, can be drilled, sawed and sanded, just like wood.

Blueing the metal parts of the gun Damaged metal parts are a little more difficult to put right. Although fairly resistant to scratching, the factory blueing on a steel barrel can wear away eventually, and this could accelerate the onslaught of rust. Again, there are no real short cuts, and once the gun becomes too unsightly for your peace of mind, the only answer is to re-blue it. In the factory, blueing is applied using heat, but cold gun blue cream can be bought from local gun dealers. This does a very acceptable job without the need for heat or messy chemicals. Take care when using gun blue though, as it is corrosive and poisonous.

With the stock removed, use a very fine 'wet or dry' paper (used wet) or else fine wire wool to remove the existing blue. It will pay to try the blue on a very small corner first, to ensure that it works on your particular gun. Some weapons have a finish which will not accept blue. Once the surface has been cleaned back to bare metal, and any rust has been removed, the whole part to be blued should be de-greased using a solvent cleaner. Methylated spirit does a good job, but use a clean, lint-free cloth to remove any powdery deposits before commencing blueing. As with any repair job, time spent in meticulous preparation will be repaid by the quality of the final finish.

Detailed instructions are provided with cold gun blue, and these should be carefully followed. The cream is applied to a small area at a time, and care should be taken to avoid going over the same area twice, as this can cause colour variation. If the colour needs to be deeper, the whole area can be covered again once the first coating has been applied.

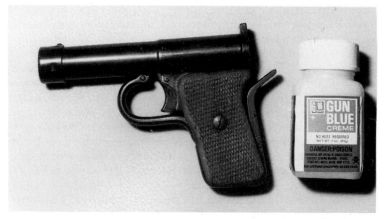

Cold gun blue gives an effective finish if care is taken in preparation.

If the preparation work was properly done the final finish should be as good, perhaps better than, the original.

Some guns have an epoxy-type black finish which can be difficult to remove, and the metal underneath may not take a blue, so try a small area first. You might need to resort to a metal scraper to remove this type of finish, but try not to score the metal itself.

Customising really is a field of study on its own. There is something deeply satisfying about creating a gun which stands out from the crowd and looks really special. Many individuals, however, do not feel that they have the necessary skills to enable them to carry out customising work, yet many small jobs can be done without the need for specialised equipment or facilities. The main point I think is to build up confidence gradually by working on scrap materials. Do not try to be too ambitious all at once, such as attempting to create elegant scrolls and hunting scenes on the woodwork. Often the simple designs and ideas are the best.

Once you have worked on a few basic customising projects, such as making new butt grips for a pistol, or revarnishing a stock, you will find that you begin to develop the self-confidence to tackle larger projects. Patience is really the key to success in any worthwhile customising project, since any attempt to hurry the job is sure to spoil the end result. I must confess that I am not always too good at following my own advice, and occasionally I am up burning the midnight oil in an effort to complete a job which I have been looking forward to showing off at a field target event the next day.

The best way to tackle a large customising job is to think of it as a collection of individual smaller tasks – it can be a little daunting to look at a rough-hewn chunk of wood and try to visualise it as a sleek custom gun stock. Take it stage by stage, and it will not seem so intimidating.

Building a Custom Stock

Let us look at the stages involved in, say, building a complete new custom stock for an air rifle, complete with inlay and varnish.

Good planning is essential to any project, and customising is no exception to this rule. Decide first exactly what you want from a new stock. Perhaps you have seen a custom stock in a gun shop or at a competition and decided it would look smart on your own gun. Remember that a custom stock should feel more comfortable in use than the original stock, and the gun should be quick to come on target. They are not designed just to look attractive, but have a positive function, too They should fit the requirements of the individual shooter better than the mass-produced article.

Try some different modified stocks if possible before you start building. Shooters at field target events are often only too pleased to have other enthusiasts admire their guns, and will usually allow you to heft the gun and feel the difference between the modified version and the standard article. The difference can be quite considerable, and can make a pleasant surprise to anyone who has not tried one before. Make sure you are fully happy with the style of stock and are going to be able to live with the design before starting work.

Selecting design Ensure also that the design of the custom stock you have in mind is appropriate to your own gun. I once built a custom stock for a BSA Mercury, using maple, an expensive, fine-figured white timber, and modelled the stock on one I had seen on another make of air rifle. After about two months of spare time work, culminating in the installation of dark rosewood inlay and ten coats of clear varnish, the stock cracked at the pistol grip the second time I used it on the gun. I gave the remains of the stock to a wood carver friend of mine to use to make small items rather than waste the fine timber. I had made the mistake of applying the wrong type of stock design to my gun. The pistol grip area was too narrow to take the strain of the cocking action of the air rifle on the large screw which lets in through the base of the pistol grip on the Mercury. It may well be, too, that there was an invisible flaw in the timber which I used, and perhaps the angle of the pistol grip was too sharp to provide the needed strength. Avoid making the same mistake by looking carefully at custom designs which have been applied to your particular make and model of gun. Follow the basic designs adding your own individual ideas. Of course, if you have one of the more unusual models of air rifle you may be very much on your own and need to experiment to achieve results. Remember the mistake which I made, and hopefully it will help you to avoid possible pitfalls at the outset.

Obtaining the wood The wood for a stock can be obtained from gunsmiths and occasionally from stalls at game and country fairs. Incidentally, these types of events are often a useful source of both materials and ideas, attracting as they do specialists from all over the country. Watch out for dates of fairs in your local county magazine or in the airgun magazines.

Of the available timbers, English walnut is the most popular, and justly so, being beautifully figured and a real delight to look at, but it is expensive. Other hardwoods can be effective, though not all are suitable. Mahogany and similar timbers are used quite often, but personally I find this type of timber tends to dent a little more easily than some. Rosewood is beautiful but splits rather too readily. It is best for inlaying, especially with a lighter coloured timber such as maple. Timber can be ordered from a specialist hardwood supplier; many timber yards deal almost solely in softwoods, and either have difficulty in obtaining hardwoods or are simply reluctant to order the small quantities required by customers.

Cutting and shaping Your air rifle will have an existing stock which has cut into it various grooves, holes, notches and so on to take the action.

These must be faithfully reproduced on the new stock, so ney need to be carefully measured and recorded. An effective way of doing this is to use tracing paper to transfer the general shape of the cut-outs to the new stock. The depths of these recesses will vary, too, so care should be taken when recording the information not to miss any detail.

First plane down the timber to give a reasonably smooth surface for marking out, then rough out the overall shape with a pencil, allowing plenty of room for final shaping and for any small cutting errors you might make. Saw out the rough shape, having first checked that the pencil markings are in the right place and that you have the correct dimensions before proceeding.

The top of the stock into which the action fits needs to be flat and square, so that the inletting may be accurately cut to take the cylinder of the rifle. This is the area to work on first using a good quality smoothing plane. Hold the stock in a carpenter's vice or Workmate to keep it steady as you work; protect the wood from the jaws of the vice with cardboard.

The actual inletting, unless you have access to expensive power equipment for specialist woodworking, will need to be carried out using hand chisels of appropriate sizes and probably a gouge. A gouge is simply a type of chisel with a rounded rather than a flat blade. Depending on the make of the air rifle being worked on, it will probably be required to cut the channel in which the cylinder rests.

A mallet will be needed for use with the chisels, too. The work will involve much testing for the fit of the cylinder in between chiselling, and you should avoid cutting too much wood off in one go – it is much easier to remove wood than to put it back. If you do take too much wood off, however, you can repair small damaged areas using a proprietary wood filler such as Plastic Wood, or you can make up a filler of your own to match the wood, using fine sawdust from the wood itself, mixed with a suitable clear or semi-clear adhesive. I have done this myself very effectively, but plenty of practice is needed to ensure an accurate match. It is far better not to take off too much wood in the first place.

One thing you will notice if you have to fill overcut areas is that these will often be a different shade, usually darker, when varnished. What looks like a good match at the time may be less so when the work is fully completed. Test first, complete with varnish, on off-cuts to be safe.

Once the action sits neatly into the new stock, any holes needed for securing screws can be drilled. Having done that, remove the action and continue shaping the wood towards the finish.

A tool called a spoke shave (a type of two-handed plane) is useful for initial shaping of a stock. Chisels and planes may also be used. At the risk of offending traditionalists in woodworking, I am going to suggest an alternative, and faster, way of achieving the final shape of your custom stock: use an electric sander, or drill with a sanding attachment (rotary), and fit a medium grade sanding disc. Use this to shape the stock carefully. Do not be tempted to use a coarser grade of disc to speed up the process, since the faster cut may cause you to remove too much wood, and the coarser discs can leave deep scoring. You may then remove too much wood while trying to get rid of the scoring. Change to a fine grade sanding disc at an early stage to avoid these problems.

The eventual finishing needs to be done by hand. This is probably the most time-consuming part of the whole process and must not be skimped. Any abrasions will show up much more prominently when the varnish is applied, even though such defects may not be noticeable at the sanding stage. A good idea is to sit down and watch television or listen to the radio as you work – it makes the job seem less arduous.

Inlaying Select whatever material you have decided to use for inlaying, be it contrasting hardwood, mother of pearl, plastic or whatever. If you decide to be adventurous and utilise unusual materials for inlaying, be careful that whatever you use will not shrink or crack when installed, spoiling the final finish.

Install the inlay in the manner described earlier in this chapter, levelling the surface flush with the stock as soon as the adhesive has dried. Once you have had practice at inlaying (it is essential to practise on scrap materials before touching your valuable stock), you may feel like having a go at creating some more ambitious shapes to inlay: animals, birds, geometric designs, etc. Modelling drills and very small wood carving tools are useful here, and you can let your imagination run riot.

You are no doubt wondering how to cut around a complex shape in detail to inlay it. What you actually do is to cut around the main shape of the inlay, as accurately as possible, but ignoring any holes and detail cuts. Inlay the piece and when set, sand down flush with the stock as before. The remaining detail is then filled using a filler which matches exactly the wood from which the stock is made. This can be made up or bought, as described earlier.

If you are using a dark timber for the stock, a substance called orange shellac, which can be ordered through chemists, may be used to do the filling. Shellac comes in flakes, and is brittle, breaking up easily with rough handling. It is used in the manufacture of traditional French polish.

Heat up the tip of an old screwdriver for about thirty seconds or so over a gas flame. Place a flake of shellac on the inlay, then apply the heated screwdriver to the shellac, which will instantly melt and fill the holes. Sand down as before.

Heated shellac can be mixed with small quantities of sawdust for a more accurate colour match, but it is unsuitable for light coloured timbers, being of a darkish brown itself.

If you prefer to use transfers rather than inlay, these can be applied after the first coats of varnish have been allowed to dry. The final coats of varnish then protect the transfer and stop it from rubbing off.

Finishing and varnishing When the final sanding is completed, the grain of the timber needs to be sealed to ensure a smooth, clear result. Before applying any sort of finish, ensure that your hands are clean, then pass them over every part of the stock. This will effectively remove any dust which might otherwise spoil the final result. There are grain sealers which can be used, but some of these impart a degree of colour or irregular marking which is undesirable when a clear finish is used.

I usually apply a single coat of varnish. Polyurethane is very durable, and there is a choice between a non-reflective silk finish or a high gloss. When this first coat has dried thoroughly I rub it down using a finishing grade of 'wet or dry' paper. As the name implies, the abrasive paper can be used wet or dry, though it does last longer and finishes more smoothly if it is used wet. This means, though, that the work must be carefully washed and then thoroughly dried before applying the next coat of varnish.

The first coat of varnish effectively fills the grain, then a succession of coats can be built up to give the desired depth of finish, rubbing down lightly to remove dust between coats. This is known as 'flatting'. The final coat should be left for a week to harden fully, and then can, if required, be treated with rubbing compound, available from car accessory suppliers. It is a mildly abrasive cream which is rubbed into a section of the stock at a time, then rubbed off with a clean cloth, having removed a microscopic surface layer of varnish, together hopefully with any surface ripples or other irregularities. Be careful not to rub too hard when using rubbing compound or you will cut right through to the wood. For this reason, it is worthwhile to finish with at least six coats of varnish, or even more. This gives you a greater depth of finish to work with, but avoid allowing surface irregularities to build up in the hope of removing them at the rubbing compound stage. It should only be necessary to remove a very fine film with the compound. The compound can then be washed off and the stock buffed with a clean dry cloth.

Next use a mildly abrasive metal polish to remove any blooming left by the rubbing compound, and after removing all traces of these materials a fine wax polish can be applied. If you have opted for a silk or matt finish, the final polishing stages can be omitted. If you have no experience of these processes, practise on scrap materials first before touching your prized custom stock.

Finish is very much dependent upon good preparation and time spent at the sanding stage will be well repaid, as will the use of a good quality brush when varnishing. When applying a clear varnish do not use a brush that has previously been used for paint, no matter how well cleaned. However, a well-used, softened brush is better than a new brush, which is best avoided unless it is of sable or similar soft hair. Even then it is likely to shed a few hairs at first.

Part of the attraction of customising is that you can use your own imagination widely and can be innovative. I think there is something of the adventurer in all of us, so customising is sure of a great future.

INDEX